IMAGES
of America

SALEM, NH
VOLUME I

Unlike today, cameras were once prized possessions. Back in 1915 when Sarah Fielding Dyke got this new Kodak, she was so proud of it that she had her picture taken with it. Many of the photographs in this book were taken with cameras just like this one. Salem owes a debt of gratitude to Sarah and to all the other early shutterbugs in town. Their snapshots of family, friends, and favorite places captured and preserved a lot of local history.

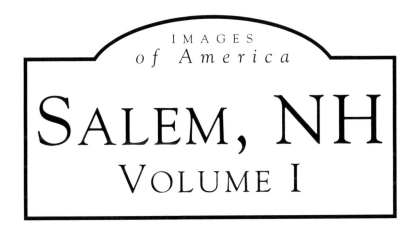

IMAGES
of America

SALEM, NH
VOLUME I

Katherine Khalife and Douglas W. Seed

ARCADIA

First published 1996
Copyright © Katherine Khalife and Douglas W. Seed, 1996

ISBN 0-7524-0420-2

Published by Arcadia Publishing,
an imprint of the Chalford Publishing Corporation,
One Washington Center, Dover, New Hampshire 03820.
Printed in Great Britain

Library of Congress Cataloging-in-Publication Data applied for

To Dad:
Thanks for the history.

Salem was called Cow Hampshire by Massachusetts folks back in 1942 when this picture was taken. Mary, Arthur, and Harry Azarian didn't mind. After all, if Salem didn't have all those cows, there wouldn't have been any family milk trucks to play in.

Front Cover Illustration: The Granite State Potato Chip Company got its start in this North Broadway building early in the century. Much enlarged over the years, the chip factory has always been a favorite of Salemites and tourists alike. Granite State's story appears on p. 121.

Contents

In 1938 the town proudly advertised itself on its 440,000-gallon water tower, built on Howard Street in 1925. The letters were removed as part of a national security effort during World War II.

Introduction

During our months of research for this book and its companion volume, one cynical soul asked why we wanted to do even one book about Salem, never mind two. "After all," he said, "the town is nothing but housing developments, traffic jams, and parking lots. What are you going to write about—the history of tattoo parlors and backyard grills?"

Attitudes like his may be exactly why books like these are needed! History needs to kick us all in the pants once in a while, if only to restore our perspective and gear up our gratitude. No, Salem isn't Concord and Lexington, but it's full of fascinating history just the same. In fact, Salem's history contains many of the same things we go out of town to learn about—things like slavery, religious intolerance, life in a Puritan settlement, the Industrial Revolution, and so much more. Getting a sense of our own history has a way of making us look at even little things differently.

Knowing, for example, that oxen used to travel down Main Street may not seem like any big deal—until you're sitting in Depot traffic some 90° afternoon. Then, at least, you can be glad you're not stuck behind one! And all those mornings you've spent clearing the lawn of litter tossed from passing cars? If this were 1826, you'd be picking up feathers—left behind by flocks of turkeys, ten thousand strong, led down the Londonderry Turnpike by unlucky drovers.

A sense of history does give life a new perspective. Sometimes it's just plain fun. Did you know that, back in the early 1950s, Roland LaRochelle had a roadside diving board next to his woodworking shop on Route 28? That way, on hot afternoons when he wasn't busy, he could spend a little time somersaulting into the Spicket.

And did you know that Edward F. Searles' craving for turtle soup led him to stock the area around World's End Pond with turtles imported from Europe? Think about that one the next time you stop to let a turtle cross the road.

These are only two of the hundreds of wonderful anecdotes we heard during our journey into Salem's past. Often, while gathering these stories, we stumbled across photographs of people and places we had all but given up hope of finding. For example, Lennie Peever's family sent us wonderful photographs of his drug store, but sadly, didn't have a picture of him inside the shop. Some weeks later, while flipping through an album at Jim Sayer's house, looking for a photograph of his Ole Rock Drive-In, there it was—druggist Lennie Peever, in his pharmacy, standing in front of a "Strike with Ike" poster in 1952. Pay dirt!

When coincidences like this happened over and over again, we realized that it wasn't coincidence after all. More often than not, people's albums are filled not with pictures of themselves, but with pictures of the people, places, and events that have touched their lives.

Tucked among a group of photographs of Fred Detlefs' 5 & 10, we discovered a snapshot of his wife's bowling league at the old Bluebird Lanes on Main Street. The two interior pictures of Woodbury High classrooms came from Danny Donabedian and Don Turner, from whom we had expected farming photographs. When we asked Wally Craig for pictures from his years at Gelt's Market, we were thrilled to find that one of them was taken in the ballroom of the Rockingham Hotel—a priceless shot now that the hotel is gone.

Capturing scenes and times now lost was our goal when we were asked to do this book and its companion volume, *Salem, NH, Vol. II: Trolleys, Canobie Lake, and Rockingham Park*. We have used current street names and addresses whenever possible, so that readers can go out and explore some of the locations pictured in these pages. We hope our two books will stimulate your interest in Salem's past and we also hope you'll read—or reread—the town's two official histories: *History of Salem, N.H. 1735–1907* by Edgar Gilbert and *At the Edge of Megalopolis: A History of Salem, N.H. 1900–1974* by Richard Noyes.

Salem has a wealth of history. It's all around us, just waiting to be discovered.

Douglas W. Seed and Katherine Khalife
June 1996

One

The Center

Back in the 1600s, Haverhill owned much of what is now Salem, Methuen, Atkinson, Hampstead, and Plaistow. Life revolved around the Puritan meetinghouse at Haverhill, which served both as the seat of town government and the tax-supported church. As the small settlement began expanding into its outlying lands, however, residents in the more remote locations found themselves out of touch with life at the townhouse. Methuen sought General Court permission to set up its own parish in 1725. The new district, which included a large portion of Salem, built its meetinghouse near today's Holy Family Hospital. Thirteen years later, wanting a town house of their own, Salem residents petitioned to become the North Parish of Methuen and built this meetinghouse at Salem Center.

It was a joyous moment when people in Salem received General Court permission to form a separate parish of their own. For thirteen years they had been paying a minister's tax to the meetinghouse in Methuen—too far away for most of them to attend. The whole village gathered on November 15, 1738, to watch the frame of the new meetinghouse being raised.

In 1741, when boundary lines between New Hampshire and Massachusetts were settled, the North Parish of Methuen found itself located in New Hampshire. The First Congregational Church remained Salem's only tax-supported church until 1819, when a new state religious tolerance law rendered it self-supporting. In 1840 the church moved out of the meetinghouse to this new building on Lawrence Road, where it remains today.

In 1893 a state incentive offered $100 in books to any town willing to expend $25 to set up a public library. Salem took the challenge and set aside a room at the town house. Eighteen months later the collection was moved to the former No. 1 School next door, where Alice Hall was photographed in 1960. She began working at the library in 1915 and finally retired in 1972, after spending the last six years of her career at the new Kelley Library.

Methodism in town dates back to 1803, when meetings were held at Jacob Rowell's house at the crest of Zion's Hill. By the time the Liberty Methodist Church was built on Bluff Street in 1809, it had 279 members. In 1836 the society divided, with one group going to North Salem and the other to Salem Center.

The church at the Center is shown here before being destroyed by fire in 1917. Salem native Charles H. Tenney, owner of Grey Court castle in Methuen, contributed $5,000 to the rebuilding fund, stipulating that the new church be named for his mother, Hannah Tenney, who had once been an active member of the church.

At first, school was held in private homes for a month or two each winter. In 1759 it was decided to hire a "riting, sifering, and reding scool master" for each of four areas of town. Schoolhouses were built in the early 1800s, with tax abatements given to citizens who contributed money or materials. When school districts were numbered in 1824, the Center became District No. 1. This building opened on School Street in 1895, and was replaced by the Haigh School in the 1950s.

Back in the early 1700s, before any roads connected the Salem lands with the principal settlement at Haverhill, a foot trail called Spicket Path served as the main thoroughfare. It ran from Haverhill, up and over Spicket Hill, to Salem Center. Because the Center became the location of the meetinghouse, it earned its status as Salem's historical heart even before the town was chartered in 1750.

The Center still looked like a sleepy village in 1907 when this panoramic photograph was taken. It looks west from atop 354-foot Spicket Hill, the town's highest point. In the foreground at left are Bridge Street and Bodwell Pond. The large barn to their right is the approximate location of today's Douglas Drive.

12

Starting at the right, beyond the meadow, are the back sides of the old public library and the meetinghouse. To their left, at the intersection of Main and Bridge Streets, are the old cemetery and Hose House No. 2.

In the very center of the panorama is the 1836 Hannah Tenney Church. Just beyond it, Main Street continues to meander toward the Depot and the hills to the west while Lawrence Road stretches to the left, becoming a pastoral landscape south of the First Congregational Church.

Traffic jams don't yet exist, nor do traffic lights. And the closest thing to a housing development is the sparsely populated area of School Street and Highland Avenue, seen at right, beyond the meetinghouse.

James Ewins was the third generation of his family to run Ewins' Store at the northwest corner of Main and School Streets. His grandfather John, a Harvard graduate, purchased it in 1805. The store had one of sixteen telephones in town when this photograph was taken c. 1902. The market contained a post office three different times before 1900, with all three generations of Ewins serving as postmaster. William Brown opened Bill's Market here in the early 1940s, and the store again served the Center's postal needs until 1965.

Volunteers proudly show off their fire-fighting apparatus at Hose House No. 2. After insurance underwriters agreed to reduce insurance rates if firehouses were built at the Depot and the Center, $1,000 was appropriated for the station. It was erected in 1906 on the cellar of an old blacksmith shop and liquor store. Now used as a town storage building, the hose house once contained Salem's police lockup, municipal offices, and public meeting space.

The cast-iron horse watering trough is gone—as are the trolley tracks—but otherwise, the intersection of Main Street and Lawrence Road is quite recognizable. At left is the original Masonic Building, erected in 1873. A post office was located there for several years, as were stores operated by Earl Gordon, A.N. Russ, and C.I. Bowker. Until 1836, wandering cows were rounded up and kept in an enclosure called the town pound, located across Lawrence Road from the Masonic Building.

Campfire Girls pose on Main Street across from Hannah Tenney Church in the 1930s. From left to right are: (front row) unidentified, Helen Brown, Betty Thorpe, Eleanor Clevesy, Ethel Tessimond, Mrs. Smith, Carol Dickey, and Phyllis Allard; (second row) Mabel Dyke, Bertha Downs, Dorothy Wadlin, Gladys Brown, unidentified, unidentified, Dorothy Ritchie, Barbara Ritchie, and Ann Bucheri; (third row) Elizabeth Haigh, Virginia Abbott, and Doris Willis; (back row) Muriel Austin and Ruth Haigh.

The brick T.M. Russ factory, built in 1886 on Main Street near Lawrence Road, was one of Salem's largest shoe manufacturers. Other shoe-related businesses at the Center included Bodwell Wood Heel on Bridge Street and a number of smaller operations in private homes. In 1900 Salem was New Hampshire's sixth largest shoe producer.

The Russ factory later found new life as the Robbins Transportation Company, egg suppliers to First National Stores all over New England. In the photograph at left, workers candled eggs before packing by holding them under a bright light to check for freshness or fertility.

In the 1970s, Udo Fritsch's U-DO Manufacturing Company occupied the building. Fritsch developed the first screw-in fluorescent light for home use. Today, Diversified Optical Products is located here.

After Leo Berard gave this house to George Taylor in 1930, Irving Lundberg was hired to move it to 56 Bridge Street. The house originally stood next to the Russ Shoe factory on Main Street. Paul Kezer (left) and Gene Wallbridge, a lineman for the electric company, helped with the $250 moving job. House moving has taken place in Salem since the town's early days, when buildings were put up on rollers and pulled to new locations by teams of oxen.

Junior Women's Club members Lelia Gordon Rowell and Florence Doble Goundrey posed in front of the Soldiers Monument on the common during a Memorial Day celebration early in World War II. The banner they held eventually contained an initialed star for each Salem resident who served. The common was the original site of the meetinghouse, which was moved to its present location in 1838. The burial ground behind the common was laid out in 1736.

Stanley Stewart's Stanwood Park was located on Spicket Hill off Bridge Street. It had a tea room and dance hall—popular in the late 1920s for check dancing (5¢ a dance) and "most beautiful girl" contests. The dance floor put a spring in your two-step, thanks to trolley springs underneath. The bandstand's backdrop was painted by orchestra leader Ben Kittredge. These members of the 1927 band are, from left to right: Doc Vose, Thomas Kittredge, Howard Goldsmith, Kenneth Morrison, Ben Kittredge, Herbert Chase, and John Crockett.

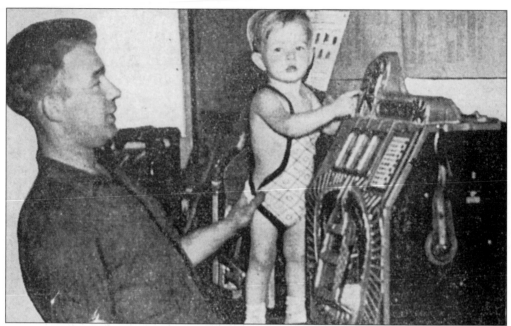

These two old *Boston Post* newspaper photographs are not of the best reproduction quality, but they show how common slot machines were in Salem during the 1930s. Even Louis George's post office (below) at 278 Main Street had one! The penny and nickel one-armed bandits could be found just about anywhere in town—diners, stores, restaurants, and barber shops all had them. Legend has it that the penny arcade at Canobie Lake Park even had a false wall to hide a row of slots when the "heat" was on! Were they illegal? Sure, but nobody seemed to care. In fact, merchants were usually warned in advance when the occasional crack-down—or robbery—was about to take place. The machines would mysteriously disappear for a day or two and then reappear right back in their old spots, cherries, lemons, and all. Even the *Boston Post* called it "all good fun."

Two
North Salem

North Salem remains today the best example of what Salem looked like years ago. Built up around the old path from Londonderry to Haverhill, the early village had gristmills and sawmills that drew business from miles around. North Main Street was laid out in 1750, and in 1769 East Broadway was built from Schultz's Corner at Zion's Hill Road. Each man worked out his share of highway taxes on the road near his land, while other workers were paid two shillings a day—more if they brought a yoke of oxen, and still more if they provided an ox cart. Nothing typified life in North Salem for much of this century better than Palmer's Store, captured above by photographer St. Linger in 1952.

Derry native William Palmer attended Salem's No. 3 School at 98 Haverhill Road. In 1911 he began his forty-eight year stint as North Salem's postmaster at his store on East Broadway. The quintessential good citizen, Palmer provided water, a playground, and custodial services to the No. 4 School, and served in the village fire company for over forty years. He and his wife Carrie are shown here in 1951 taking a break to admire the "catch of the day." The two boys are their grandsons, Ralph and Bill Ermer.

A peek inside Bill Palmer's general store shows him proudly displaying the new line of Admiral televisions and radios for 1951. Like most stores of the time, space was at a premium and wares were stacked wherever there was room. Behind Mr. Palmer is the North Salem Post Office. A barred window and a few mailboxes mounted in the wall served the area until April 1995, when the post office was enlarged into the barn portion of the building.

Looking in a southerly direction, this pre-1907 postcard shows the intersection of North Main Street and East Broadway. The image was captured from a spot near the North Salem Methodist Church. Straight ahead is North Main Street, which bends left to travel south along today's Arlington Pond. Around the corner to the right, on East Broadway, are the North Salem Fire House, Palmer's Store, and the No. 4 School, later renamed in honor of William Palmer.

The North Salem Methodist Church was built next to the site of Taylor's Store in 1836. The church was enlarged to this appearance in 1864, but was destroyed by fire forty-five years later. When the $1,000 insurance pay-off was not nearly enough to rebuild, church members sought help from Methuen millionaire Edward F. Searles. His $5,000 contribution came with the stipulation that he be allowed to design the new church, which still stands today.

While farm work and fresh air kept most Salem residents healthier than their crowded Lawrence neighbors to the south, there were still public health concerns in town. With no hospital, most Salem babies were born at home. Outhouses, especially at schools, were always a problem for the board of health; intestinal diseases were the fourth leading cause of death back then. Pneumonia, tuberculosis, diphtheria, and typhoid were also frequent threats.

Doctors were often non-existent in Salem. Dr. Lewis F. Soule came to town in 1898 at the request of selectmen. Three years later, Dr. Vladimir Nicholas Sikorsky (left), the son of a Russian nobleman, settled in North Salem.

Sikorsky and his family lived at this house on old North Main Street, which sits today under Arlington Pond. One can only wonder what local Yankees thought when he advertised the place as Dr. Sikorsky's Salem Sanitarium for Nervous and Mental Diseases. Business evidently wasn't very good, as the sanitarium closed in 1905 and Dr. Sikorsky moved to 293 Main Street at the Center. His new home was an old meetinghouse moved here from Windham by coffin builder Jonathan Pettingill.

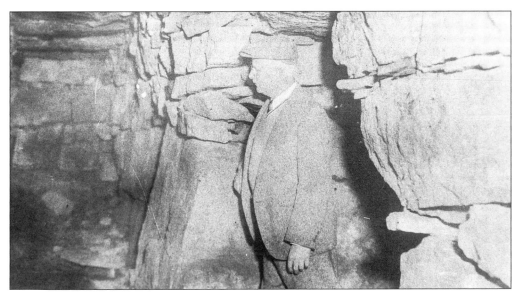

America's Stonehenge is a fascinating 30-acre site off Haverhill Road. It contains underground chambers, astronomically aligned granite monoliths, and an ancient "sacrificial table" weighing 4.5 tons. So say the believers, anyway. The doubters say that the stone structures are nothing more than storage areas built by nineteenth-century farmer Jonathan Pattee. Pattee's Caves, as non-believers call them, were acquired in 1936 by William B. Goodwin of Hartford, Connecticut, who tried to discern the origin of North Salem's mysterious stones. Unfortunately, Goodwin (shown above in the Oracle Chamber) used such crude excavation techniques that much evidence was destroyed. The site was purchased in 1957 by Robert E. Stone of Derry, who is shown below posing at the sacrificial table a few years later. He operates the enigma as a tourist attraction while continuing the research. Although modern radiocarbon dating methods have shown artifacts from the hill to be some 4,000 years old, the debate continues.

One of North Salem's most unusual houses was built before 1920 as a summer residence by Thomas Sharpe, a Methuen tea merchant. Located on Dow's Hill, south of Cowbell Corner, the Haverhill Road property was the former site of an old tavern and cider mill. Sharpe started his Globe Tea Company with a horse and wagon in 1888, traveling door to door selling home-blended teas, coffee, butter, and provisions. With a good mind for business, he was soon using his profits to invest in property along the Eastern seaboard. Looking for a location to build a summer home, Sharpe was struck by the pastoral setting and beautiful view from the Haverhill Road hilltop. He purchased the land and constructed Sharpehurst, a stone cottage surrounded by a low fieldstone wall.

Thomas Sharpe, a familiar figure around the area, is poised behind the wheel of his right-hand drive 1913 Buick, traveling from his Methuen home (above) to North Salem. Beside him in the front seat is son Thomas Sharpe Jr., while his wife Jane, daughter Gertrude, and son Reginald ride in the back. The Sharpes eventually had six children in all.

Thomas and Jane Sharpe relax at Sharpehurst in 1934. While they never became year-round residents of Salem, their son Thomas Jr. did, settling on Lawrence Road in 1927. Thomas Sharpe III was a Salem police officer for many years and his sister, Eunice Sharpe Girard, still lives in Salem today. The fourth generation Thomas Sharpe is currently a Salem fireman, as is his brother Stephen. Sharpehurst was sold about 1940 to Dr. and Mrs. Harry Kellett. They enlarged the home and eventually lived in it year-round.

North Salem was once a bustling industrial area with small mills producing shingles, shoes, flannel, lumber, gloves, matches, and woolens. The Spicket River provided water power and remnants of some of the old dams, canals, and mill ponds remain today. Taylor's Mill, located on the east side of North Main Street opposite the church, was once the town's largest woolen mill. It employed one hundred people when this 1870s photograph was taken. Fire destroyed the factory in 1878.

Tucked away in the extreme northeast corner of town sits Cowbell Corner—the junction of East Broadway, Haverhill Road, and Derry Road. Its unusual name comes from a small bell that once hung in the belfry of a nearby woolen mill. The Spicket River splashes noisily into Salem here, passing under a bridge just south of the intersection. North Salem's first post office opened near the corner on June 15, 1831, with Nathaniel B. Duston as postmaster.

Three
Lakes and Ponds

Salem's bodies of water cover only a few percent of the town's 16,384 acres. Hard to believe when you consider the number of people who have splashed, jumped, paddled, and fished in them over the years! Whether natural or man-made, Salem's six lakes and ponds have provided recreation, income, drinking water, food, ice, home sites, and lazy summer afternoons to generations of Salemites and out-of-towners alike. By the time Engine No. 3674 pulled into Canobie Lake Station in the 1930s, cottages had been dotting the shore for fifty years and Canobie Lake Park was in full swing. The town's other lakes were rapidly becoming vacation havens, too.

Known as Haverhill, Polis, then Policy Pond, Canobie Lake received its new name in 1885 when the railroad station was built at the southeast corner of the intersection of Route 111 and Old Rockingham Road. Early the next year, Albert O. Alexander became postmaster at the new Canobie Lake Post Office, located in his store across Route 111 from the station. The building burned about ten years later and Alexander constructed this new store in the same location.

By 1932, Robert Mason had updated A.O. Alexander's General Merchandise store to look like this. The transplanted Methuen native sold Socony gasoline, groceries, and camping supplies to thousands who ventured north on Route 28 looking for summer fun. A Republican, Mason became the Canobie Lake postmaster in 1925. He held the job for nine years—until Roosevelt's administration appointed a Democrat and the post office moved to the store across the street.

A c. 1932 glimpse inside Mason's Store reveals something for everyone. Tonic from Hill's of Methuen was available from the machine next to the scale, and Granite State potato chips were dispensed from the glass case on the lunch counter. Red salmon was 19¢ and Boston papers blared the headline, "Kiss and Tell Cop Bares Story of Affair with Jessie." Mason's son, Robert Jr., took over management of the market in 1956, modernizing it substantially. The business was sold in 1972 and renamed Canobie Market.

Gurry's Store sat across Route 28 from Mason's, at the northeast corner of that road's intersection with Route 111. This photograph was taken c. 1940, three years after Grace Gurry became the Canobie Lake postmaster—a position she held until the post office was discontinued in 1963. A modern glass-front lunch counter was added in the 1950s. After Gurry's closed, the building was home to Sea 'N Sirloin and Bonico's restaurants, but has been unoccupied for the past few years.

The first real cottage development on Canobie came in the 1890s when George P. Cross laid out sixty-nine small lots on the lake's southeastern shore. Policy Pond camp (left) was built in 1893 by L. Wallace Hall. Its lumber once comprised the boiler room walls of a wood heel shop in the Depot. Hall, a descendant of the first Caucasian child born in Salem, grew up in Boston where he later practiced law. In 1913 Hall was appointed Salem's judge, a post he held until 1944.

The small dam by the rowboat's bow serves as the outlet of Canobie Lake. The resulting stream is Policy Brook, which meanders some 4.5 miles through town. Known as the Flume, the area is located on the Lovers' Walk that led from Canobie Lake Park to the hotel on Canobie Avenue. The downstream side of the Flume became a popular swimming hole after 1903, when public bathing in the lake was banned. The cottages and path are now gone and overgrown.

Although Allen Bean, Albert Fisher, and Randolph Miller had great fun with this 1926 Model-T Ford on frozen Canobie Lake, ice was serious business in town. In the days before electric refrigeration, ice houses existed on most of Salem's lakes, storing hand-cut blocks that were delivered door to door by horse-drawn ice wagons. Home deliveries of block ice continued right up into the early 1960s, when some summer cottages still relied on antique ice boxes to keep food fresh.

Long before Lawrence's Arlington Mills built a storage reservoir on Hitty Titty Brook in 1917, the area around Bluff Street at the southern slope of Zion's Hill was known as Millville. The hamlet may have gotten its name as early as the 1700s, when wood for the meetinghouse was cut at a sawmill there. One of the other small factories located at Millville was G.M. Woodbury's shoe shop, shown here on Bluff Street in the 1890s.

With the creation of Millville Lake by the Arlington Mills in 1917 came a shoreline ripe for summer home development. Lawrence merchants and businessmen began to erect cottages there in the early 1920s. Like most camps of the times, they had broad porches to catch the breeze, boats for fishing, and pumps and outhouses for life's other necessities. Genevieve cottage was built in 1927 by Lawrence carpenter Samuel Lemay for his daughter and son-in-law, Genevieve and Carl Inacker. Three generations of the Lemay family enjoyed the home, which was turned into a year-round residence in the 1930s. These photographs, taken on July 18, 1929, show Samuel's son Cyril and son-in-law Carl with the day's catch (above), while Samuel plays with his grandchildren on the shore (below).

Irene Frazier stopped for a photograph outside Seubert's Store at Millville Lake, c. 1950. Ruth and William Seubert, owners of a bakery on Jackson Street in Lawrence, purchased a camp on Millville Circle in the late 1920s. They converted it to a year-round home with beautiful landscaping, even including a large stone fish pond in the design. The couple were familiar figures at Millville, riding their horses there each morning.

When the dance hall (below) burned, they saw the opportunity to open a variety store on the site. Located where the town beach is today, it served the Millville neighborhood for many years. Five generations of the Seubert family enjoyed life at the lake.

Although Arthur Marden eventually owned much of Millville Circle, Henry Morrison was the first developer at the new lake. He changed the name from Hanagan's Pond and posted red arrows all over town pointing the way to his camp lots and dance hall, shown here in 1925. Engineer William E. Lancaster reportedly surveyed the lots for free—after losing a bet that Morrison wouldn't find any buyers for his campsites. Henry's wife, Bessie M. Morrison, became Salem's first woman selectman in 1969.

Back in 1659 Shadow Lake was called Satchwell's Pond, for the Haverhill surveyor who "discovered" it. Native Americans, of course, already knew about it. They called it Hitty Titty, which remained its official title until about 1913, when the name was changed to Shadow Lake. In 1907 there were only three cottages at the lake; by the late 1920s there were enough to warrant a dance hall and a neighborhood store. The Shadowland Store, shown above *c.* 1932, had become Shadow Lake Variety by the time the photograph below was taken in 1959. Joseph and Rita Lafontaine owned a farm in Pelham before purchasing the store in 1955. It came complete with its own beach across the street, which they continued to open free to the public every summer. Soon after they sold in the early 1960s, a private beach association was formed. The store, now a dwelling, still stands on the east side of Route 111 at Sylvan Drive.

Frank Lundberg's busy ice house stood on a peninsula at the southeast end of Shadow Lake. Ice blocks were originally cut by horse-drawn ice plows and later with large hand saws. They were floated to a steam-driven conveyor (above) that carried them up to the storage house. Stacked between thick layers of sawdust, the well-insulated 320-pound blocks would stay frozen for months. In good years, two harvests were possible—one early in the winter, another early in the spring.

Listed as Copls Pond in 1723 records, Captain's Pond may have taken its present name from Captain James Webster, who settled on Hooker Farm Road before the Revolution. The area was once so remote that residents escaped Indians by gathering in a block house on Liberty Street. The farm shown here is now the site of an upscale housing development; Gibson's Beach once stood near the large barn. Trailblazers, YMCA, JCC, and YWCA day camps have also been located at Captain's Pond.

Submerged at the bottom of Arlington Pond, just north of the dam, are the ruins of John W. Wheeler's textile mill. A mill site since before 1750, the property was purchased by Wheeler in 1860. After suffering two fires—and two rebuilds—he opened this brick structure for the manufacture of flannels and blankets in 1881. Another fire prior to 1909 finally destroyed the business once and for all.

In 1920, the powerful Arlington Mills of Lawrence bought the remains of Wheeler's Mill, along with 350 acres in North Salem. Here, the factory sits waiting for demolition—as part of the grand plan to dam the Spicket River and create a billion-gallon reservoir. Successful completion of the project would assure a steady flow of water to keep Arlington's downstream looms producing year-round.

This scenic section of North Main Street, photographed in 1907, now lies at the bottom of Arlington Reservoir. Relocated to its present route c. 1920 to make way for the impending flood, all that remains of this road section now is Arlington Pond Court and Wheeler Dam Road. When the lake was drained in 1983 to facilitate dam repairs, the old road was found—in such good condition that it was used to bring in heavy equipment needed for the dam's refurbishment.

Along with Wheeler's Mill and North Main Street, some fifty homes, an electric generating plant, and thousands of trees fell victim to the huge Arlington Reservoir project. In the foreground is the old timber dam that held back the Spicket to form Wheeler's mill pond. Across North Main Street stands the soon-to-be-demolished John W. Wheeler residence. The 1881 brick mill building shown at the top of p. 36 is behind the camera that captured this image.

Not since Lawrence's Great Stone Dam was built in 1845 had the area seen an engineering project of this magnitude. The huge Arlington Dam rose 48 feet from the Spicket River's bed. A 550-foot concrete-cored dike was built some distance to its east, and a smaller, earthen dike was built to the west. Trees cut from the reservoir site yielded over a million feet of lumber— some of which was used as framing for the concrete work.

Construction of the Arlington Dam and reservoir took most of three years to complete. It was finally filled in the spring of 1923, turning what was once a large part of North Salem into an underwater ghost town. The dam immediately became a popular spot for picnics, sightseeing, and maybe even a little "necking" after dark! Three pretty Salem girls posed on the dam *c.* 1940. From left to right are: Carrie Donabedian Tomasian, Vera Avedisian Garabedian, and Dorothy Donabedian Derohanian.

This 1925 view looking west speaks volumes about growth in Salem. Where virtually no trees appear in the photograph, tall pines and dwellings abound today, and the downstream side of the 735-foot dam is now overgrown with trees and brush. A development scheme, which named the newly created shoreline Arlington Park, encouraged the rapid multiplication of summer camps around the lake. A 1941 report claimed that Nazis planned to dynamite the dam. They didn't—and all remains well in North Salem.

Four

Crossings

The steel ribbons of the railroad came to Salem in 1849. As the tracks marched northwest from the state line, running parallel to Route 28, they passed across several existing roads at the south end of town. The neighborhoods around the resulting intersections became known as Messer's, Kelley's, and Cluff's Crossings—taking the name of each area's nearest or most prominent neighbor. The history of South Salem and its crossings may not be as well known as the history of other parts of town, but it is equally as fascinating. It was here that Salem's only Olympic champion grew up. It was here that Robert Frost taught school. And it was here that a Methuen millionaire built a stone-walled kingdom.

The area around the junction of Route 28, Hampshire Road, Lawrence Road, and Hampshire Street became known as Messer's Crossing—taking its name from the enterprising Richard Messer family who bought a house on Pond Street in 1765. The railroad tracks crossed Hampshire Road just west of Route 28, and a station was built at the crossing in 1855.

This turn-of-the-century photograph was taken from behind Hillcrest Road, looking south toward the station. As the only place in the vicinity where kids could see the "inside of the earth," the ledges in the picture were a popular play spot. Being so close to Massachusetts, people who lived at Messer's Crossing had Methuen telephone numbers and usually went south for church and shopping. Before Salem built its high school in 1925, it wasn't unusual for neighborhood residents to go to Salem only twice a year—to pay their taxes and to attend town meeting.

The crossing, its station, and the double-track siding that once served a freight house were photographed from the south by Carlton Parker in 1932. Remnants of the station can still be seen today. The house and barn to the northwest across Hampshire Road belonged to Frederic D. Tootell, whose Hampshire Roads Electric Company brought the first electricity to South Salem. His oldest son, F. Delmont Tootell, brought Olympic gold to Salem in 1924, winning the hammer throw competition at the Paris Olympics.

David Messer built a tavern on the still-existing triangle at Route 28 and Hampshire Road in 1816. A lively place for dances and shooting matches, it was a favorite of cattle drivers on their way down the Londonderry Turnpike to Boston slaughterhouses. Some of the cattle met their fate right at Messer's, in a butchering house on Hampshire Road. David's brother lived across Route 28 from the tavern, in an old house that Lavington Dyson bought in 1893. Dyson and his family (above) posed there in 1899, next to the wagon he used to deliver milk to Lawrence boarding houses. Just southeast of the Dyson place, facing Hampshire Street, was the Heaps Brothers' Blacksmith Shop (below), built by David Messer c. 1872. The Heaps boys were sons of John B. Heaps, who ran a store at the Point A trolley station off Raymond Avenue.

By the 1920s, Messer's Tavern on the triangle was long gone. It was destroyed by arsonists in 1896, after being renamed the Buffalo House and gaining notoriety for liquor raids and other goings on. Dyson's old house across the street was gone, too, but his sons Lavington and Raymond had new homes on the site. Lavington's house and store, on South Broadway at Pond Street, is shown here. Both brothers' homes were replaced by a shopping plaza in the early 1980s.

Poet Robert Frost earned $24 a month teaching several terms at the one-room No. 9 School at 224 Lawrence Road. During Christmas break in 1895, he married his Lawrence High co-valedictorian, Elinor White. Eight years later, students at the No. 9 School posed for a photograph. From left to right are: (front row) Arthur Dyke, Raymond Dyson, Jim Herron, Albert Townsend, Master Jagger, Hazel Kelley, and Rachel Kelley; (back row) Lavington Dyson, George Luther, William Herron, Theron Butler, teacher Ms. Peabody, Elizabeth Dyson, Eva Vartanian, and Evelyn Dyson.

42

Sarah Fielding Dyke and Helen King stand guard at the state line marker on Hampshire Street about 1905—on the lookout for Massachusetts interlopers, no doubt. Sarah's house, across the street from the marker, straddled the state line, requiring her family to pay taxes to both Salem and Methuen.

This photograph was snapped at the same Hampshire Street marker about fifteen years later. This time, Hannah Heap, Albert Townsend, and Roger Townsend—all unarmed—pose on Albert's motorcycle. The field in the background was part of Townsend's farm. Today it is the location of the large Oak Ridge Avenue apartment complex.

Brindle, Ebony, Speckle, and Bess were on their way back to George Townsend's barn on this afternoon in 1916. Townsend started his Sand Hill Road dairy in 1901. It was destroyed by fire more than fifty years later. Almost every family had a cow before daily home deliveries of milk began in the 1890s. By 1912, more than two dozen Salem families were in the milk business. The number of cows in town topped out at 836 in 1940.

Albert Townsend had one of the first motorcycles in Salem, and probably the very first one with a side car. He returned from gunning one day in 1916, showing off a wild duck. Wild birds and animals abounded in Salem back then. Fox were plentiful and herds of deer grazed regularly on the side of Route 28. Wolves were so numerous in colonial times that at a 1766 town meeting residents voted to pay $10 for each one destroyed.

Certainly the most intriguing figure around Messer's Crossing was Stillwater estate owner Edward F. Searles. As locals looked on with suspicion, jealousy, or disdain, Searles swept into town in the mid-1890s, buying up property that eventually totaled almost one-tenth of all the land in Salem. Born in Methuen in 1841, Searles rose from a boyhood job in the Methuen Cotton Mill to a career as an interior designer. After working in Boston, he obtained a position with Herter Brothers, a prominent New York firm. The company's clients included San Francisco's Mrs. Mark Hopkins, widow of one of the Central Pacific Railroad's "Big Four." Society gasped when Mrs. Hopkins, sixty-eight, married the forty-six-year-old Searles in 1887. The couple settled at Edward's Pine Lodge in Methuen, where he became a widower four years later—inheriting almost $22 million.

Searles' Stillwater acquisitions in Salem centered around World's End Pond. Considered the end of the civilized world by Haverhill pioneers in the 1600s, the pond's still waters were being consumed by mud and vegetation when Searles came on the scene. His plan to naturally dredge World's End—by routing the flow of the Spicket through it from the northwest—was foiled when Ozro Butler refused to sell him the farm on which Barron School sits today.

The Messer's Crossing area was most likely the site of the first house ever built in Salem. The neighborhood owed its early origin to its location on the Dracut Path, the route between the settlements at Haverhill and Dracut. Part of the old trail was made a Methuen highway in 1735, eventually becoming today's Pond Street and Hampshire Road.

The earliest homes disappeared long before Edward Searles came along, but some Messer's residents watched uneasily as he moved, dismantled, or altered several mid-eighteenth-century dwellings in the process of assembling his estate. He even rerouted roads when it suited him: for instance, after acquiring the Thomas Webster house (at left, in the background), Searles decided that it sat too close to Pond Street, so he simply diverted the road away from the property. He died in 1920 and this part of Stillwater later became Law's Dairy. Today it is the site of a housing development.

The first of Searles' Salem lodges to be constructed was Meadow Brook at 67 Pond Street, built as a caretaker's house in 1896. Gates, still standing to the left of the house today, mark the location where Pond Street once curved off to the north. At one time, artist Arthur E. Lowe was the caretaker in residence here. Searles shared his love of art and would visit regularly, arriving in a chauffeur-driven Pierce Arrow.

Westmoreland Lodge (above) was constructed in 1897 as a home for the estate's cook. The huge greenhouses, now gone, were part of Searles' plan to make Stillwater self-sufficient. Westmoreland's address is 277 Lawrence Road, but it was positioned to face the road shown above, which once ran east off Lawrence Road to Pond Street. The 90-acre property was purchased for $7,500 in 1924 by Armenian immigrants Edward and Araxie Manoogian. Westmoreland and the other Stillwater properties were enclosed by Searles' characteristic stone walls. Seen below at their early stages in 1898, they eventually extended from Pond Street, up Lawrence Road, and east to Oak Hill Farm, now the site of Northeast Rehabilitation Hospital on Butler Street. By the late 1920s, when huge portions of the walls were being destroyed by thieves, the Manoogian family and other owners put many of them up for sale.

Searles dotted Stillwater with picturesque stone towers, arches, and bridges. This one was photographed in 1910. Many of them can still be seen today, in the bushes off Lawrence Road, and Pond and Butler Streets. Sadly, the estate's beauty was not meant to be shared, as it was hidden behind high walls and foreboding No Trespassing signs. Even World's End Pond was blocked off to public access. Many of Searles' actions spawned resentments that made some Messer's residents vow never to sell to him.

The construction of Stillwater Manor, the estate's Pond Street centerpiece, began in 1898—the same year that Searles persuaded the B & M Railroad to change the name Messer's Crossing to Hampshire Roads. Like most of Searles' buildings, this one was designed by Henry Vaughan, original architect of the National Cathedral in Washington, D.C. Incredibly, the manor housed its master for only one summer, when a broken leg reportedly kept Searles from moving on. Today the building is divided into condominiums.

Kelley's Crossing, about a mile north of Messer's, is the spot where the railroad tracks passed over Kelley Road, just a few yards west of Route 28. The planked crossing, typical of those in rural areas, was located a few feet east of Benjamin Kelley's farm. Shown here in 1920, the B & M line shoots north from the crossing like an arrow, toward Salem Depot. The pastoral view is a reminder of an era void of shopping plazas and rush hours.

The Benjamin P. Kelley homestead on Kelley Road, just over the tracks from Route 28, was built in 1863 by Jonathan Ballard. Kelley bought the place in 1881 and it stayed in the family until 1955. When Ben died, his horse Nellie knew the route to follow through Methuen and Lawrence for the family's door-to-door produce business. Above, Nellie stands with Ben's son, Arthur G. Kelley, who willed $25,000 toward the construction of Salem's Kelley Library.

Farmers and railroad men alike knew the nasty effect a locomotive's cow-catcher could have on stray animals. This stone tunnel under the B & M line allowed Benjamin and Arthur Kelley's livestock to safely move east and west without crossing the tracks. Located between Kelley Crossing and the Spicket River, the tunnel is typical of many in New England.

Allan Dearborn paused at the Kelley Road bridge in 1920 to appreciate Policy Brook serenely flowing below. One has to admire the ingenuity and efforts of our forefathers for building such strong and stately stone bridges with the means they had available to them. This old bridge even withstood the torture of heavy automobiles and trucks until nearly the middle of the twentieth century, when it was replaced with a modern concrete structure.

Aptly named, Egg Rock stood in the middle of the Spicket River where it passed through the Kelley farm. After Benjamin Kelley passed away, his son Arthur named their acreage Egg Rock Farm in honor of this beautiful scene. Thanks to seventy-five years of vegetation and population growth, this section of the river is now remotely located somewhere southeast of the Haigh Avenue housing development.

The Kelley family enjoyed bicycling, a wildly popular form of transportation at the turn of the century. There were twenty thousand bicycles on the nation's roads in 1884; more than ten million by 1895. Watchmakers, jewelers, and booksellers even began going out of business as Americans spent their extra money at bicycle shops instead. Gathered here are, from left to right: (front row) Lena A. Kelley and Mildred Kelley; (back row) Maggie C. Kelley, Benjamin P. Kelley, Eva V. Kelley, and Arthur G. Kelley.

Cluff's Crossing was named for the Cluff (or Clough) family who had owned property near the site of the railroad tracks since 1683. August and Anna Dietrich, German immigrants, moved to the area in 1895, purchasing 20 acres on the north and south sides of Cluff Road at Route 28. They posed in front of their home (above) with oldest daughter Esther and son Albin about 1899. That same year their property tax bill (below) was $17.51. The family sold produce and blueberries in Lawrence each summer and cut ice in the winter at their pond. They were best known, however, for the white Emden geese they raised. The birds, which graced many a holiday table, took prizes at country fairs for over sixty years. The family sold the home in 1989, after ninety-four years at Cluff's Crossing.

Preserve this Bill and bring it with you when you call to pay your tax.	
REMIT STAMP IF YOU WISH BILL RETURNED.	

SALEM, N. H.

Incorporated May 11, 1750.

Poll Taxes are due on presentation of bill.

Six per cent. discount on all taxes paid prior to Oct. 1, 1899.

Non-Resident Tax not paid Dec. 1, 1899, and Resident. March 1, 1900, will be advertised.

RATE, - $19.20 per $1,000

FRED O. WHEELER, Collector.

Post Office Address,

BOX 82, - SALEM, N. H.

Salem, N. H., June 1, 1899.

Agust Deitrich

Your Taxes for 1899, are as follows:—

DIST. No. *8*   DIST. No.

State, County, Town and School Tax,   *17.51*

Schoolhouse Tax, - - -

Highway Tax,   **1899**

Amount,   -

Discount, - - -

Interest, 10 per cent. after Dec. 1, 1899,

Dec 2   Received Payment,

F O Wheeler

by F O Wheeler Collector.

The Collector will be at Page's Blacksmith Shop near Hampshire Road Station, to receive Taxes, on Sept. 27th, from 1 to 4 P. M.; at the residence of R. F. Wheeler, Broadway, Salem Depot, Sept. 28th, from 1 to 4 P. M.; at Hanson's Mill Office, North Salem, Sept. 29th, from 1 to 4 P. M.; at Town House, Sept. 30th, from 9 A. M. to 4 P. M.; and on the first Saturday of each month from Sept. to Feb. next, from 2 to 3 P. M.

Every Fourth of July, August Dietrich made a big batch of homemade ice cream for his five children to share with the Kinzler kids—as shown here in 1910. William Kinzler (second from right) grew up to serve the town for forty-seven years, first as an elected road agent and later as head of the highway department. The former Kinzler homestead at 21 Cross Street now houses the Salem Public Works Department.

Twenty-nine-year-old Albin Dietrich became a Salem police officer in 1923 and stayed involved for the next forty-eight years. The same year that Dietrich joined up, Fred Chrysler became acting chief—a post he held until his death in 1944. Salem's officers posed for this photograph in 1925. Chief Chrysler sits astride the department's only vehicle, an Indian motorcycle. Behind him stand, from left to right: Ralph Haigh, Howard Davis, Albin Dietrich, Clarence Wadlin, and Herbert Hilberg.

Teacher Mary Webster stood in the doorway of the No. 8 School on Cluff Crossing Road at South Policy Street when this *c.* 1905 photograph was taken. The students are, from left to right: (seated) unknown, Alfred Findeisen, and Albin Dietrich; (middle row) Nozing Garabedian, Dora Peters, Gertrude Metzner, Martha Hird, and Nancy Hird; (back row) Amy Young, Esther Dietrich, Maud Curtis, Mary Young, John Hird, Parker Nichols, William Kinzler, and Mildred Kelley.

The building shown at the top of the page was constructed in 1801. Several schools were built that year, pushing the town's total school taxes to $1,528, up from $315 the year before. Teachers' salaries rose accordingly, up from 1800's grand total of $217.76. The one-room schoolhouse was replaced in 1907 by the new No. 8 School shown here. Soule School opened next door as its replacement in 1962, but Salem's rapidly growing population kept No. 8 in use until 1967.

Five
The Depot

SALEM N H

The Manchester & Lawrence Railroad, which became a branch of the B & M in 1887, changed the face of Salem. Before its arrival, much of the area around the intersection of Main Street and Route 28 was farmland. Once the railroad came through, however, growth began moving away from the now-bypassed Center and North Salem, toward the spot where the tracks crossed Main Street. The first train depot was located in an old house on North Broadway, but it soon moved to the north side of Main Street next to the tracks. The station above was built as a replacement in 1867 and the village of Salem Depot sprang up around it. By the time this photograph was taken in 1911, the Depot was the new hub of town.

A tranquil Salem Depot is detailed in this artist's rendering, published in 1887 by George E. Norris of Brockton, Massachusetts. The intersection of Main Street and Broadway is in the lower right and the high hills of North Policy Street fade off to the northwest in the upper left.

Unlike today, dwellings lined the west side of Broadway from Main Street south. The industrial area north of the Depot was a flourishing complex of manufactories that hugged the rails of the B & M.

Thriving here in 1887 were the Evans Artificial Leather Company, an oxalic acid factory, a thread mill, F.P. Woodbury and E. Roswell's shoe factories, Bailey's heel shop, and Livingston's planing mill.

The crossing of two main roads also brought with it a wide variety of grocers, blacksmith shops—and even Napoleon Senecal's combination meat market and billiard parlor!

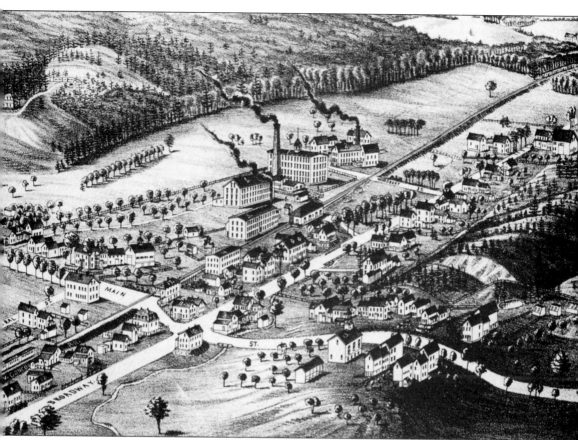

A brook mysteriously appears, flowing south from under Main Street, just east of Broadway. At one time, this stream powered a saw and gristmill that was located just a few hundred yards up Broadway from the Depot, near the industrial buildings. The stream eventually dried up to a degree that made it useless for water power. The building was then converted into Union Block, containing four tenements, a shoe shop, and a meeting hall. The Pleasant Street Methodists held their earliest meetings there, and school was held there during the week.

The brook still flows today—piped under the entire Depot area—resurfacing behind Dunkin' Donuts and the Coca-Cola bottling plant.

A sharp eye will notice how much land is void of trees. At one time, farmers had cleared 80 percent of New Hampshire's land; today the state is 80 percent wooded!

Double iron crossed Main Street to serve both the station and the industries above the Depot. The crossing gates were operated from the small, maroon and yellow building at right, which was removed in the late 1950s. The station is the second on this site—the first having been moved to Windham Junction to serve as a freight depot. The boxcar in the distance is on a siding at Salem's freight house, which became the Dodge Grain Company in 1954.

Frank "Pop" Bemis served as railroad agent from 1921 until 1953, when passenger service ended and operations moved to the freight house up the tracks. The station was purchased the next year for $4,000 by Attorney James A. Sayer Jr., whose law office still remains there in 1996. Grossman's Lumber, not yet in Salem, advertised Swedish Venetian Blinds and "slam-tested" Genasco roofing materials. Other posters included one for Boston's Manger Hotel, boasting 500 rooms at $2.50 and up, with bath.

Railroad crossing gates frame this winter scene of Main Street looking west, *c.* 1930. At left is the drug store of Amos J. Cowan, who began his trade in Salem in 1915 and sold to Orlando Abbott twenty-five years later. In the center is the home of Dr. William Greer and, later, of Dr. Harry R. Kellett. The intersection of Main and Pleasant Streets was Salem's "medical center" for more than forty years, with Doctors Kellett, Greer, and William Land on opposing corners.

This view is similar to the one above, but it was taken in 1906. The building on the left houses Dr. Soule's drug store and street railway waiting station. Built in 1895 by Fred Buxton, the structure would serve not only Dr. Soule, but also Cowan's and Abbott's pharmacies, plus several other businesses over the years. Here, where the streetcar tracks crossed the B & M railroad line, many hair-raising moments were experienced as trolley drivers raced through the crossing to beat oncoming trains.

A Massachusetts Northeastern streetcar heads east through Salem Depot, *c.* 1910, past George H. Webster's store and barber shop (right). The building on the left, remembered by most as Joseph Low's Market, housed many grocery stores over the years. J.C. Carey had Salem's first telephone there in 1881, and A.M. Rolfe's delivery horse served double duty pulling the fire wagon for Hose House No. 1, located next door on Main Street. Imagine the square today if the horse-watering trough was still there!

Few details are to be found about this horrible auto wreck at Salem Depot early in the century. It is known that the trolley was not involved and had just stopped to look over the wreckage. One report claims that the car belonged to a band leader who had come to Salem for a performance. Whatever the circumstances, this was undoubtedly the worst auto accident ever seen by on-lookers of the era.

When the trolleys left Salem in 1929, busses began rolling through town to take their place. By the summer of 1932, Mason's Canobie Lake Coach Service was running eighteen trips a day from Lawrence to Canobie Lake Park, at a round-trip fare of 25¢. Driver Leonard (Lindy) Collupy, shown here in 1935, was a familiar figure around town. He was a bus driver for many years, first for Mason's and later for the Hudson Bus Lines.

Liquor was nothing new in Salem when the Blue Front opened at the southeast corner of Broadway and Main Street sometime after 1907. Rum was a particular favorite in the early days. Back in the 1700s, the town often supplied a few gallons of the stuff every time a road was being built. When the temperance movement was in full swing in the 1850s, selectmen-appointed liquor agents were the only ones who could dispense spirits—for medicinal purposes only, of course.

By 1861 the new village at the Depot felt the need for a church of its own. Isaac Emerson of Melrose, Massachusetts, donated a lot on Pleasant Street and within a few days enough money was pledged to plan construction. The new Methodist church opened on July 1, 1862, with twenty-five members. By 1865, membership had increased enough to raise the minister's salary from $300 to $500 a year and purchase a lot at Hedding Camp Ground in Epping.

Church played a large part in most people's social lives. In addition to still-popular suppers and fairs, there were summer Bible schools and social clubs for teenagers and adults. The Methodists had their Epworth League while the Congregationalists and Baptists had Christian Endeavor Societies. Church sports teams, like Pop Allard's Pleasant Street K.K. Class basketball team, were favorites, too. The players in this 1923 photograph are, left to right: Loren Ross, Ralph Littlefield, Bertie Blois, Eugene Allard, Onester MacLean, and Earle Magoon.

Leo Bergeron (below at right, in 1933) had his first experience at barbering in his father's busy nine-chair shop on Hampshire Street in Lawrence. By 1933, after working in New York, he was in business for himself at the Salem shop shown in these two photographs. Leo's was one of the best spots in town to share the latest gossip or even strike a deal. It's said that customers did everything but hold court there. In 1946, for example, thirteen World War II veterans gathered at Bergeron's for the first meeting of Salem Memorial VFW Post 8546. His building, which sat between Pilgrim Block and the train station, was demolished in the 1970s—twenty years after Leo sold the shop to Nick Santangelo.

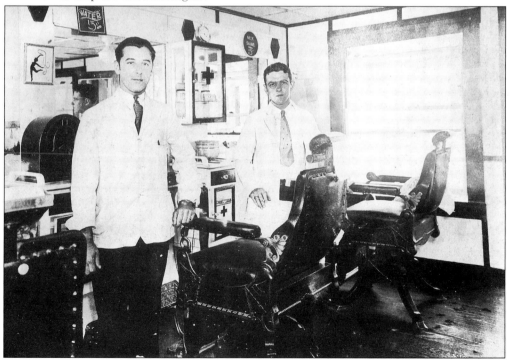

The Rockingham Hotel, built at Main and Central Streets in 1880, was one of the largest commercial blocks in town. Among a number of businesses located there was a grocery store, owned by W.J. Brown when this *c.* 1903 photograph was taken. The store changed hands several times, and eventually W. Earle Magoon managed an A&P market at the hotel. Pictured above are, from left to right: Sarah Davis Pease, Gertrude Cole Quimby, Lena Bailey Kelley, Woodbury Brown, and Joe Breckles.

The hotel got this new look in 1906 when Rockingham Park was about to open for the first time. The building was enlarged and upgraded in anticipation of the many wealthy bettors expected to visit during the racing season. A ballroom and extra guest rooms were added, as was an elegant entrance on Central Street. Unfortunately, gambling was permanently shut down on the second day of racing, leaving the hotel's new rooms practically empty.

One of the busiest tenants in the hotel block was Fred C. Buxton. Not only did his newspaper store contain the Depot's post office, but Salem's American Express office as well. When the number of telephones in Salem climbed to sixteen in 1902, Buxton added the town's telephone switchboard to his shop, with the operator selling candy and magazines between calls. And when there were finally enough automobiles in town to warrant a gas pump, one of those was installed, too.

The hotel ballroom hosted many events over the years. One of the most eagerly anticipated was the annual Food Fair put on by Gelt's Market to benefit the Salem Fire Department. People who attended received not only free samples from the displays set up by Gelt's suppliers, but also the chance to win one of fifty food baskets loaded with donated goodies. At this early 1950s fair, long-time Gelt's employee Wally Craig greeted guests in the center of the hall.

Salem Depot abounded with markets. One of the longest-lived belonged to Benning Noyes, across the street from the Rockingham Hotel. Early every morning Benning and his right-hand man, Forrest Palmer, would begin filling orders to be delivered during the day. Since pre-packaged foods were not yet common, everything from sugar to lard had to be weighed out, wrapped, and tied with string. Like many establishments of the time, Noyes even sold kerosene, pumped into 5-gallon cans from a tank at the back of the store. At first, deliveries were made by horse and wagon or horse-drawn sleigh. For a short time, Benning instituted a Motor Store (above), taking the market right to the customers. Charging groceries was common back then and in tough times people often couldn't pay on time—if at all. Legend has it that Noyes once burned $10,000 worth of uncollectible grocery accounts.

Benning Noyes and his wife, Anna Smart Noyes, played a major role in the development of Salem as we know it today. Anna moved here from Derry and first worked as a bookkeeper for the trolley company. She later was the Salem reporter for the *Lawrence Evening Tribune* and the night supervisor at the Salem Telephone Exchange. The couple were both active in Salem's Board of Trade and saw the town's potential as a suburban bedroom community. They became one of the first to establish a business on Route 28 when they purchased White Bridge Inn and opened Ann's Fried Chicken Restaurant in the early 1940s. At the same time, they began to develop Noyes Terrace, one of the town's earliest housing developments, on the Inn's acreage between Lawrence Road and South Broadway.

In 1941, Noyes constructed a new commercial block on the site of his store and the land adjacent to it to house his market and Orlando Abbott's pharmacy. By the time this photograph was taken in the mid-1950s, Abbott had sold to William Galloway, Benning had passed away, Forrest Palmer had taken over the market, and Anna Noyes was serving in the New Hampshire Legislature as the first woman ever elected from Salem. During her term she married local selectman and representative Howard Willis.

Gus Brown's family bought the Wilson Brothers General Store at the Rockingham Hotel in 1923. They moved to this building a few doors east after a fire at the hotel two years later. Brown Brothers sold everything from meat to paint, and Gus often had to leave customers waiting as he ripped off his apron and ran out to drive the town's only firetruck. The building to the left of the market, later moved to 7 Pleasant Street, once housed the town offices.

Route 28 was two-lane Rockingham Road when this 1938 view of the Depot was taken. The building next to Brown Brothers Market is at left, on the southwest corner of Main Street and Route 28. Just beyond it on the northwest corner is Pilgrim Block, built in the mid-1800s. It housed stores on the first floor and a public meeting hall above. In the foreground at right is the building where Gelt's Market would settle in a few more years.

This rare photograph, passed down through the Hall family by Judge L. Wallace Hall, shows a fascinating c. 1905 view of the building that later became Gelt's Market on Route 28. As the liquor store of LaCourt and Tuttle, it specialized in Portsburger Ales and Lagers. To its right sits a c. 1905 automobile with butterfly fenders and bail-handled lanterns. Behind the car, most interesting of all, is a large sign advertising Bill's Wild West Show.

George Gelt opened a market on Main Street in 1938 when he was twenty-one years old. Two years later he bought a building on Route 28, enlarging it to this appearance by 1954. A later renovation modernized the store into a supermarket. Wally Craig, who worked at Gelt's for thirty-two years, became a partner in 1960 and the sole owner in 1976. The market closed on December 31, 1978, and the building was razed to make room for the new Salem Co-Operative Bank.

Leonard B. "Lennie" Peever came to Salem in 1927 to work at Keating's Drug Store. He purchased the business the next year, gave it his own name, and operated it until 1974. Peever (left) and George Gelt pose here during their 1960 duel for a seat on the board of selectmen. Gelt, who operated the supermarket next door to Peever's, won the election. Lennie would earn his seat in the 1963 race.

Peever and Gelt were just two of a long line of Salem businessmen who volunteered their time and talents to serve in town and state politics. A short list of them includes: Fred C. Buxton, John W. Turner, Henry P. Taylor, Charles A. Kimball, Wallace W. Cole, Frank D. Wilson, Charles H. Borchers, Arthur M. Rolfe, William A. Croft, and William A. Brown.

A landmark for generations, Peever's Drug Store stood guard over Salem Depot for forty-six years. The building, which at different times housed the Blue Front, Webster's Barber Shop, and Keating's Drug Store, became Peever's in 1928. Traffic has plagued the intersection since the advent of the automobile. In 1974, upon Peever's retirement, the town bought the land and rounded-off the corner—leaving only a small grassy area to remind us of the site.

A staunch Republican, Lennie Peever paused next to his "Strike with Ike" poster in May of 1952. Since he represented Salem in the New Hampshire General Court for seventeen consecutive terms, attended four Constitutional Conventions, served as a selectman, *and* worked as Salem's first dog officer and health officer, Lennie's store became the place to go for spirited political debate. It's said that more political deals were struck at Peever's than at the statehouse!

Fire ravaged Peever's Drug Store in 1941, but Lennie was up and running again in no time. In 1951 the store was completely remodeled again—this time with an all-new, modern facade, a new soda fountain, and a new name; Peever's Drug Store was now a pharmacy! One look at the building's proximity to South Broadway (right) and Main Street shows why the town was so eager to use the land to round-off the corner in 1974.

In high school, John Castricone pumped gas at George Blois' service station. It became Johnny's Shell when Castricone bought the business in 1958. In 1967, he razed all the buildings on his Salem Depot corner and Shell built him a brand new station. Salem Attorney Bill Mason, who pumped gas there while he was in law school, bought the business in 1978. The property again changed hands—and brands—when Mike Papageorgiou reopened the station as Mike's Sunoco Ultra Service in 1993.

"Poultry Feeds To Make Your Hens Weigh, Lay and Pay" was the theme of C.F. Kimball & Sons' float in the town's 175th anniversary parade in 1925. After selling their farm to the builders of Rockingham Park in 1905, the Kimballs moved their grain business to North Broadway and built this grain elevator just north of Main Street. The business was eventually sold to the Worthmore Grain Company and managed by third generation Charles L. Kimball, who later worked for Dodge Grain.

Fred Detlefs was a fifteen-year manager for the S.S. Kresge department store chain, predecessor to K-Mart. He struck out on his own in 1949, opening the Salem 5 & 10 in the former Kimball's Worthmore grain store. Fred and his wife Agnes ran the 5 & 10 for eighteen years, before selling the property to Indian Head Bank for a parking lot in 1967. The bank, which later became Fleet, was located in the old Salem Trust Company building further north. Attached to the north side of Detlefs' store was space that housed the town offices from 1949 until the mid-1960s. At the 5 & 10 (now a generic name, no longer referring to nickel and dime prices), shoppers could buy everything from bras to breadboxes, hair nets to Hula Hoops. Anything you really needed was probably available at the 5 & 10!

Diner food was part of everyday life in America and Salem was no exception. Across from the Coke plant stood popular Lou & Bill's Diner, operated by Lou Bunker (shown here) and his father-in-law, Bill Smith. In later years, the Steak Diner and Amanda's Restaurant occupied the location.

The Depot was always a great place for a good cup of Joe and a blue-plate special, served up at diners like Ryan's, Cross's, the Bluebird, or the Rockingham. A stretch of Route 28 south of Kelley Road was also a good bet, with the Monarch Diner, Joe's Restaurant, and Gussie's Lunch.

In the basement of the old Cowan's Drug Store building—later Bluebird Chambers apartments—were the Bluebird bowling alleys, operated at the time of this photograph by Phil Kalil. This ladies league, c. 1960, included, from left to right: (front row) Louise Porier, Hazel Blaisdel, Clara Johnston, Kathleen Merrill, and Jean Bagnell; (second row) Helen Merrill, Jessie Wadlin, Alice Taylor, and Geraldine Schofield; (third row) Phil Kalil, Agnes Detlefs, Marjorie Cain, Harriet Ford, Olive Taylor, Claire Sayer, and Miriam Robinson. The two women in the back row are unknown.

Six
Main Street

A road from Salem Center to the Depot was first laid out in 1737. Once just a dusty path—with a sunken bridge near the land that would someday hold the trolley company's car barn—Main Street grew up to be the town's major east-west thoroughfare. Farms lined most of its route for almost two centuries. In the days before the Civil War, slaves on the Underground Railroad to Canada found refuge at one near the northeast corner of Geremonty Drive. Like good Main Streets everywhere, ours has seen its share of parades, politics, public buildings—and progress. When Fletcher Gage, Ed Rolfe, and Loren Bailey drove these oxen toward the Depot, could they even imagine what Main Street would look like today?

At left, Policy Street shoots up the hill toward Canobie Lake Park while, in the distance, Main Street gently rises to meet it. The diagonal road in the foreground is gone—now part of the Fisk School parking lot. Today, the house in the middle would be sitting on Main Street in the Policy, Main, and Pelham Road intersection. It was moved to 56 Pelham Road in 1961 when Main Street was run right through the site to accommodate Interstate 93's Exit 2.

The No. 6 School got its start on the northeast corner of Main and North Policy Streets in 1801. In 1825, the town gave the building and $300 to John Merrill, in exchange for the stone house located at the point formed by the two roads. That served as the No. 6 until 1873, when a brand-new building opened on Main Street at Sullivan Avenue. When fire destroyed that one in 1894, a $4,400 replacement was built on the same spot. Students posed there in their classroom in 1911.

The No. 6 School's most famous alumnus was poet Robert Frost, the only boy wearing a hat in this c. 1885 school photograph. His mother, Belle Frost (behind him to the right), moved the family to Salem from San Francisco after her husband's death in 1885. Mrs. Frost taught at the No. 6 and her daughter Jeanie (third from left in the front row) was also a student there. The Frosts moved to Lawrence when Robert was a sophomore at Lawrence High. The No. 6 was later named for him and remained in use until 1958.

The only Roman Catholic church services held in Salem before 1909 were at the home of Mr. and Mrs. Denis Sullivan. When Father John McNamara came to serve Salem in 1910, he had neither a church nor a rectory. The Sullivans and Thomas Devine purchased and donated a house on Main Street. Its barn was detached and renovated in 1913 to become the original St. Joseph's Church (shown here). The present stone church was constructed in 1929 and St. Joseph's School opened thirty years later.

Salem was without a doctor in 1898. Selectmen put out a request and Dr. Lewis Soule, fresh out of Bowdoin Medical School, answered—beginning a local medical practice that lasted until his death in 1942. Before buying one of Salem's first automobiles, he was a traditional horse and buggy doctor, often making emergency house calls in the middle of the night—in his nightshirt, with only coat and galoshes added.

Jessie Bleakney came to Salem as a nurse for one of Soule's patients after working in West Virginia, where she treated coal miners during the 1917 influenza epidemic. She and the doctor married in 1922 and raised two sons, Lewis and Herbert. They are shown here outside their Main Street home in 1931. After Dr. Soule's death, Jessie worked as Salem's school nurse until 1966. Her son Lewis grew up to become the town's legal counsel.

After returning from World War II with a Bronze Star earned at the Battle of the Bulge, Bob Goundrey and his wife Ruth bought this house at 42 Main Street in 1949, converting it to Salem's only funeral home. Before the Salem Fire Department began providing emergency ambulance service, it was Goundrey who furnished it. When the department took over, he donated the first ambulance and was made an honorary fireman. He also served as chairman of the fund-raising drive to build the Salem Boys Club.

When insurance underwriters insisted on fire stations at the Center and Depot in 1905, Wallace W. Cole, a selectman and state senator, built Hose House No. 1 and donated it to the town. Still located near the northeast corner of Main Street and Route 28, the building was just large enough to garage this wagon, driven by volunteer fireman Charles E. Merrill, father of Salem developer George E. Merrill. Charlie the horse was a volunteer, too; his regular job was pulling Merrill's butcher cart (see below).

Sixteen-year-old Clarence W. Merrill Sr. poses in front of his brother's butcher cart in 1913. Merrill would pull up to a customer's door, take their order, and cut the meat right in the back of the cart. Charlie the horse knew the route so well that, on stormy days, Merrill could take a streetcar home and Charlie would get back on his own. This photograph was taken in front of Merrill's store, later Low's Market, at the northeast corner of Route 28 and Main Street.

On-street parking was no problem in the Depot in 1937. Gelt's Salem Cash Market was offering haddock and salmon at 29¢ a pound and, next door, the windows at the Granite State Electric Co. displayed the most modern electrical appliances. The large Odd Fellows building, now the Masonic Temple, was built in 1927 by member-investors—some of whom actually lost their homes when the organization faltered.

Elected constables and then a small, selectmen-directed police force served Salem's law enforcement needs until 1955, when money was requested for a full-time chief and four permanent officers. Justice of the peace courts prevailed until a municipal court was established in 1915. This courtroom photograph was taken when both the police station and the court were located in the Masonic Building. Money was appropriated for the present police station in 1963. The court moved to the old town hall and Frost School before assuming its new home in 1982.

The 175th anniversary parade in 1925 was the perfect opportunity to show off the town's first firetruck. Following it was a new Best tractor—Salem's first piece of heavy equipment. In the distance stood C.H. Borchers' lumber business, located in the building that would eventually house Grossman's. Borchers was Salem's fire chief and chairman of the 1924 committee formed to buy the gleaming new truck—and then figure out where to house it.

The firetruck committee invited fifty citizens to a meeting about the housing problem and more than half agreed to assist in financing a new station. When the construction bids came in, the committee decided they were too high—and in 1925 proceeded to build the station themselves. The town bought it shortly thereafter. Located at the corner of Main and Millville Streets, it served for forty years, retiring when the current station opened. It was later razed to make way for a bank.

This tree toppled on Millville Street near Main during the hurricane of September 21, 1938. The storm ripped into town unexpectedly and, within minutes, cherished elm trees were snapping like match sticks.

At Rockingham Park, where winds tore roofs off stables, jockey Warren Yarberry was blown off his horse in the second race. Canobie Lake Park was carpeted with fallen trees and clean-up efforts all over town took months. A government decision was made to store storm logs from Salem, Derry, Pelham, and Windham in Canobie Lake. Guy Ackerman was made chairman of the project and a portion of the lake was cordoned off. In retrospect, the solution may not have been wise, but the state was buried under 1.5 billion board feet of downed timber! A few Salem houses were built with storm lumber and some of the stored logs remain in Canobie to this day.

Minstrel shows like 1945's *Servicemen's Showboat* were popular entertainment—as much fun for those who participated as for those who attended. Often held at the Masonic Building or the Woodbury High auditorium, they were organized by churches, civic groups, and clubs. Al Raymond, a local singer and radio performer seen in the center of the front row, frequently directed the shows. They featured songs and skits, and always had at least one number done in blackface—a holdover from the original minstrel shows of the mid-1800s.

A Baptist Society started in Salem in 1780, thriving until the death of its founder and preacher, Reverend Samuel Fletcher, fifteen years later. Meetings were held only occasionally after that, usually at the Methodist meetinghouse on Bluff Street. In 1858 the First Baptist Church of Lawrence started a mission in town. Within seven years a dozen Salemites had officially organized into a church, holding weekly services at Pilgrim Hall. In 1869 this building was constructed at 122 Main Street. The steeple and belfry were given by Levi Woodbury in 1906, in memory of his parents. A new building on School Street was dedicated in 1973 and the former church now houses a restaurant.

From July 1902 until March 1929, Salem served as a hub in a vast system of streetcar lines. Above, a Massachusetts Northeastern Street Railway trolley car pauses on Main Street at the corner of Church Avenue. The operations and maintenance heart of the trolley system was the huge Salem Car Barn at 179 Main Street, built in 1902. Large enough to house thirty-six streetcars inside, the building also contained a foundry, an electrical substation, a paint shop, and the company offices. After sitting empty and neglected for some thirty years, the car barn was purchased in 1958 by Paul Garabedian, to house his thriving construction company. The Garabedians, who still own the property today, spent years getting the historic structure back in shape. It's shown below in 1964, during an office renovation. A complete history of Salem's trolley era is detailed in this book's companion volume, *Salem, NH, Vol. II: Trolleys, Canobie Lake, and Rockingham Park.*

Louis Wefers attended Lawrence Evening High School, where his talent on the school newspaper soon led to a forty-seven-year career with the *Lawrence Eagle Tribune*. He moved to Salem in 1944 and married reporter Rita Roberge three years later. She became the *Tribune's* Salem reporter, but with five children born in five and a half years, the couple often shared the Salem beat. The Wefers were the town's Lawrence media connection during Salem's biggest growth years. Louis died in 1971 and Rita retired from the paper in 1980.

The Nostradamus of the whimsical postcard trade offered up this Salem Depot of the Future card in about 1910. With the growing popularity of the automobile and the amazing advances in flight taking place at the time, the prophetic futurist envisioned a Salem flourishing with new technologies. Though personal dirigibles and a direct subway to New York may not have become reality, the Interstate Highway System and jet aircraft have fulfilled his vision to a great degree.

Back when the phone company thought we couldn't remember a seven-digit number, we simply dialed TWinbrook 8-2669 to reserve a table at Guy Ackerman's Ballroom. Built in 1955, the 154 Main Street function hall was the scene of untold numbers of wedding receptions, civic functions, political events, banquets, and other get-togethers. Two of its most popular uses were ballroom dancing and bingo. Ackerman's saw dozens of bands entertaining thousands of couples at regular Saturday night cabarets. The Tony Brown and Frankie Kahn orchestras from Lawrence were popular headliners. Since bingo was illegal in Massachusetts until the 1960s, busloads of players rolled into Salem from as far away as Boston for games at Ackerman's and St. Joseph's Church. The Kiwanis Club ran the bingo games at the Ballroom, raising a great deal of money for civic projects like the Salem Boys Club, opened in 1964.

Popular weeknight events at Ackerman's included big-time professional wrestling, provided by the World Wide Wrestling Federation's New England circuit. Wrestlers like Killer Kowalski, Lou Albano, Crazy Luke Grahm, Professor Turo Tenaka, and Gorilla Monsoon met with deafening cheers and boos as they dueled to the three-count.

A 1960s TV show called Hullabaloo was franchised around the country and the teenage nightclub soon came to Ackerman's—white-booted go-go dancers and all. The blaring rock and roll music was so loud that these "Hullabaloo Scene Speaking Pads" were provided with pencils at each table.

Political rallies were a tradition at Ackerman's. In 1964, presidential hopeful Nelson D. Rockefeller, then governor of New York, campaigned there. He shared a belly laugh with Evelyn D. Seed, one of Salem's pioneering women in business. A long-time member of the Salem Board of Trade (predecessor of the Greater Salem Chamber of Commerce), Mrs. Seed was the first woman to receive the organization's Nice Guy of the Year award—a few months before her death in 1979.

TV's HULLABALOO scene

Speaking Pad

A groovey kind of place strictly for teens

Joseph E. Pellerin came to Salem from Lawrence in 1941, purchasing a 50-acre farm at 147 Main Street for about $4,000. He posed for the photograph above with his son Romeo a year later. In 1953 he sold the property to Romeo, who continued to farm a portion of the land for a few more years. One of the tastiest features of farm life was the maple syrup made in the sugar house (below) every spring. Members of the family gathered near the "maple water" tree in 1957 to check on nature's progress. From left to right are: George Larocque, Andrew Pellerin, Yvonne Pellerin, Marie Claire (Larocque) Pellerin, and Ann Pellerin. The farm was sold in the 1950s to George Merrill, who developed it into 114 house lots known as Centerville Acres. Plaza Gardens Apartments are located on the former site of the farmhouse.

For the first 175 years of Salem's chartered existence, the town had no high school. In 1901, the state passed a law requiring communities with no secondary schools to provide for education in an adjacent town. Most Salem scholars wishing to continue past the eighth grade then went on to Methuen High, with Salem picking up the annual $40 per student tuition charge. Many kids, like these photographed in 1907, commuted to Methuen by streetcar, paying reduced student fares.

By 1915, momentum was building for construction of a high school, but cost concerns kept appropriations from being made. When overcrowding at the No. 1 and No. 6 Schools prompted plans for a small seventh and eighth grade building in 1924, fate stepped in to give Salem the high school it had been waiting for.

Levi Woodbury, a Salem native who made a tidy sum operating Washington's Saint James Hotel and a fleet of Potomac steamboats, offered to contribute $50,000 if the town would wrap a high school around the four planned rooms. A special town meeting approved and the brick building on Main Street opened in September 1925, four months after Woodbury's death. The high school gave teenage life in Salem a new air of excitement that still prevailed in 1938, when Warren Law and Paul Bucheri were snapped in Mr. McPhee's chemistry lab.

The new high school was a wondrous place, boasting eight rooms with facilities to teach everything from domestic science to physics, manual training to typewriting. Work had scarcely begun on the building when the decision was made to also include an auditorium, raising total construction costs to a whopping $110, 890.17.

Students, like those pictured here in the first cooking class, got busy planning all the activities Salem teenagers had been deprived of for so long: class elections, field trips, school dances, and sports teams. Francis Geremonty, a popular teacher at Woodbury, whipped baseball and football teams into shape at practices held on the Wood Heel lot at Salem Depot. Team members car-pooled to away games or traveled in the back of Mr. Cornwell's truck—outfitted with plush seats removed from old trolley cars.

The members of Woodbury's 1926 football team were, from left to right: (front row) D. Matson, M. Allard, S. McLean, E. Herbst, E. Dexter, and ? Lyons; (middle row) C. Smith, C. Dunkley, J. Morgan, N. Harrison, J. Bowyer, F. Huggins, J. Steavens, B. French, and C. Marshall; (back row) F. Lord, L. Ebert, E. Parker, W. Palmer, E. Allard, K. Merrill, coach Francis Geremonty, R. Lundberg, N. Terpsten, L. Brown, and J. Sayer. Raymond Lundberg (fourth from right in the back row) died the next year. The school newspaper was named *The Ray* in his honor.

Girls' sports were not overlooked at Woodbury. Members of the basketball team, decked out in snazzy new uniforms, lined up for this photograph *c*. 1926. The team was coached by home economics teacher Marion Turner, a young Salem woman who was fresh out of Plymouth Normal School when Woodbury opened.

Teacher-coach Francis Geremonty (at left in the front row) departed Woodbury shortly after this 1928 baseball team photograph was taken. He returned to the school in 1956, however, serving as principal until his death in 1963. Geremonty Drive is named for him. Members of his team were, from left to right: (seated) C. Dunkley, W. Palmer, C. Smith, R. French, L. Ebert, and Isaac Watts; (standing) unknown, J. Sayer, G. Spires, L. Brown, J. Bowyer, H. Harrison, and C. Marshall.

Eighth graders pose outside of Woodbury in 1933. From left to right are: (front row) F. Call, F. Radulski, G. Bourdelais, D. Webb, H. Finch, L. MacLean, W. Croft III, R. Smith, and L. Nutting; (second row) O. Pettingill, C. Coutuer, S. Bonney, L. Sevigny, D. Cornwell, M. Copeland, O. Robertson, E. Wheeler, E. Braddock, E. Fielding, R. Griffin, S. Mazurenko, and S. Dozibrin; (third row) G. Braddock, G. Levere, L. Wadlin, G. Richardson, E. Woodbury, M. Haigh, H. Woodbury, E. Bagnell, M. Ludwig, S. Bucheri, J. Spires, and K. Rowell; (back row) G. Chrysler, A. Packard, F. Nelson, L. Miller, R. Barron, B. Haynes, W. Webster, H. Frazier, and W. Hoffman.

Woodbury High auditorium was the scene of many community events over the years, including annual talent nights sponsored by the board of trade and lavish musical revues staged every February to benefit Cub Scout Pack 160. Scoutmaster William Blaine wrote and directed Pack 160 shows for almost twenty years and a dedicated committee of workers pitched in to bring them to life. When Salem High School opened in 1966, the scout shows moved to the auditorium there. This show took place in the auditorium in 1968.

Seven

Around Town

By the last quarter of the nineteenth century, Salem was getting jealous. The water power of the Spicket couldn't compete with that of the mighty Merrimack and the town watched enviously as the young city of Lawrence swelled with river-driven factories. Wanting a piece of the pie, Salem voted in 1879 to grant tax-free status to any major business settling in town. It didn't work; in 1902 animals still outnumbered people by almost two and a half to one. By 1915, a promotional brochure was advertising "a limitless supply of pure water," cheap building sites, and 'round the clock electric service. That didn't do the trick either. For the time being at least, Salem farmers would continue working their land and Frank Lundberg (above center) would keep running his Lake Street sawmill.

John Turner worked in the Lawrence mills before buying a farm on Kelley Road in the 1880s. By 1898, the family was doing well enough to purchase a much larger farm on Brady Avenue, making daily milk deliveries in the wagon shown above. For the next four generations, the Turners continued dairy farming. John's grandsons, Howard and John, each eventually concentrated on different parts of the business; Howard ran the farm while John processed and delivered milk. At the height of home delivery, Turner's Dairy had twenty-six trucks on the road, depositing glass bottles of milk and cream on area doorsteps. As other Salem farms turned into housing developments in the 1950s and '60s, Mountain View persevered. Today, golf carts, not cows, meander over the property, but next door, Turner's Dairy continues to thrive. Now processing almost 1.5 million pounds of milk a month, Turner's is one of only three pasteurizing plants left in the state.

Besides dairy farms, Salem had a number of orchards. Many raised Baldwin apples—a variety developed by eighteenth-century engineer Laommi Baldwin, who introduced them to New Hampshire at Richard Pattee's Lawrence Road tavern c. 1804. Local laborers posed above in the orchards at Mountain View farm, where 1,000 apple trees dotted Brady Avenue. The orchard's largest apple crop occurred in 1944, when the federal government purchased the excess and shipped them to war-ravaged England.

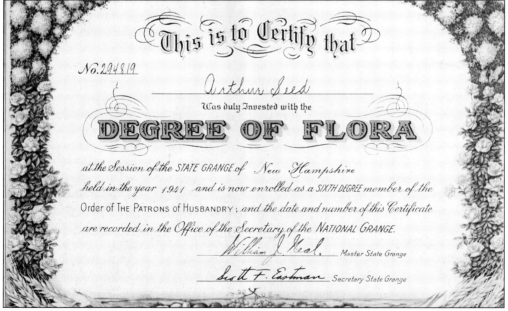

The Masons were the first fraternal organization in Salem, forming in 1868. Before long, there were Pilgrim Fathers, Odd Fellows, Daughters of Liberty, Good Templars, and many more. Nothing, however, won the allegiance of more Salemites than did the Patrons of Husbandry—the Grange. A national organization formed in the 1870s to foster agricultural interests, it was the first secret society to admit both men and women. Salem members once totaled several hundred, but the last of the town's three Granges disbanded in 1992.

At the end of the nineteenth century, hundreds of thousands of Armenian Christians were killed at the order of Turkish leader Abdul Hamid II. Many of those lucky enough to escape the massacres and death marches made their way to America—some bearing scars and tattoos of the genocide. A few of those families settled on the farmlands of South Salem, beginning in 1898. By late 1912, they resolved to build a church on Salem Street where they could maintain and preserve their culture and traditions. Shown above just as construction was completed, the Ararat Congregational Church held its first service on July 25, 1913. Services, preached only in Armenian for the first forty years, became bilingual in the mid-1950s—a few years before the photograph below was taken. In the late 1960s, a decision was made to preach entirely in English.

The cast members of this Ararat Congregational minstrel show are, from left to right: (front row) S. Vartanian, L. Danielian, M. Vartanian, S. Vartanian, H. Kachadorian, unknown, D. Donabedian, and M. Vartanian; (middle row) A. Avedisian, N. Garabedian, S. Garabedian, C. Kachadorian, V. Garabedian, V. Danielian, L. Donabedian, W. Vartanian, H. Vartanian, V. Garabedian, M. Danielian, B. Kachadorian, J. Danielian, M. Garabedian, and Sylvia Vartanian; (back row) S. Donabedian, A. Vartanian, G. Kachadorian, V. Donabedian, B. Danielian, M. Vartanian, A. Kachadorian, N. Asadoorian, R. Avedisian, A. Goergizian, unknown, C. Garabedian, and unknown.

In 1931 Edgar and Genevieve Turner opened this roadside stand at 40 Cross Street, where neighbor Sadie Bean (above) often visited. The Turners later opened a vegetable stand, expanding to a full-service variety store in 1951. Son Eddie Turner Jr. and daughter Mary Somma operate Turner's Variety today. After tacking on six additions, the family built a new building in 1973—from plans created as a Salem High drafting-class project, spearheaded by the Turners' grandson, David.

Diamond Dairy got its start when Peter Azarian's father moved to Zion's Hill in the 1890s. At first he walked to his mill job in Lawrence, but he later drove a horse and wagon, delivering milk on the way. The family moved to 51 Cross Street after Peter was born in 1900. Oddly enough, Diamond Dairy's barn never saw a cow; the company bought its milk from local farmers. In 1917 Azarian bought the first motorized milk delivery truck in the Merrimack Valley, an REO shown off above by Alice Nalbandian. More often than not, it broke down somewhere around Hampshire Road and had to be rescued by a horse-drawn wagon. By the early 1930s, when Peter posed with his wife Rose and oldest son Arthur (below), Diamond Dairy's trucks were rolling with regularity. The business continued for another fifty years, closing in 1984.

Ever wonder how Town Farm Road got its name? The credit goes to this property at No. 47, which housed Salem's paupers from 1844 until 1905 when they were sent to the county farm at Brentwood. With no welfare in existence, selectmen—who until 1960 also held the title of Overseers of the Poor—faced the dilemma of what to do with the destitute. Before the town farm system was used, contracts for paupers' care were auctioned to individual citizens, at prices determined by work ability.

Englishman John B. Heaps (back row, right) came to Lawrence to set up machinery at the Arlington Mills. Before long, he purchased a large tract of land on South Policy Street—part of which would eventually be used for the Point A trolley interchange and Heaps' Store. Every summer, friends and family weekended in a pine grove on the property. They set up colorful tents, had a special cookhouse, and put on elaborate entertainments. Members of the Heaps and Bowyer families posed there c. 1900.

It took until 1964 for postal operations at Salem Center, the Depot, and Canobie Lake to be consolidated under one roof at a new facility on Main Street, across from the present fire station. Workers gathered there in 1968 for a retirement salute to Jessie Sullivan Gallant (center), who started postal work shortly after her husband, Patrick Sullivan, became the Depot's postmaster in 1944. Her son John, who is next to her in this photograph, succeeded his father in 1950, becoming assistant postmaster of the new office in 1964.

These members of the Salem Police Association in 1948 are, from left to right: (front row) William Hoffman, Clarence Wadlin, Arthur Abbott, William Barron, Walter Haigh, George Dickey, and Maurice Haigh; (second row) Henry Morrison, Raymond Taylor, Douglas Seed, Myron Smith, Walter Vartanian, Walter Duston, and Clare Junkins; (third row) Charles Myers, Richard Kimball, John Packard, Albert Reynolds, Francis Nelson, Walter Stickney, and Philip Brown; (back row) Albin Dietrich, Thomas Reardon, Charles Ermer, Daniel Lewis, Boyce Martin, William Magoon, and Arthur Morrill.

Salem's first housing developments sprang up after World War II in the Taylor Street area and here, on Ann Avenue in Noyes Terrace. Anna and Benning Noyes constructed a few homes on the street early in the 1940s, but had difficulty finding buyers. That was no longer the case by the time of this 1950 photograph. By then, Salem was in the first stage of a building boom that would raise its population from 4,800 in 1950 to over 20,000 by 1970.

The new two-room No. 9 School opened at 287 Lawrence Road in 1925. When the first Noyes Terrace residents attended in the 1940s, there were only enough students to fill one room. By 1955, there were so many children that four more rooms were added, only to be outgrown nine years later when additional classroom space had to be set up at Mary Queen of Peace Church. Cub Scouts, Blue Birds, and Camp Fire Girls are shown here at a tree-planting ceremony in 1960. Today the building houses the Salem Senior Center.

Born in 1901, Howard E. Turner operated the family's Mountain View farm at 79 Brady Avenue until his death in 1984. His life-long love affair with Salem reached its zenith in 1973, when he volunteered to chair the committee publishing Salem's 1900–1974 town history book, *At the Edge of Megalopolis*. He also initiated the idea of capturing the memories of other older residents on audio tape. The recorded interviews became known as Project Perpetuate and the cassettes are preserved at the Kelley Library.

Howard is shown here manning a table at a mid-1970s Rockingham Park trade fair—ready, willing, and able to talk town history with anyone who was interested. The last line of the sign reveals his deep feelings about establishing roots in one's hometown.

Jim Doyle, of Andover, Massachusetts, opened the Northeastern Gliderport on a portion of Turner's farm in June 1962. For the next thirty-one years, residents admired the graceful beauty of powerless sailplanes overhead, silently soaring on thermals created by the asphalt parking lots on Route 28. In July of 1967, actors Steve McQueen and Astrid Herron came here for the filming of the motion picture *The Thomas Crown Affair*. Since 1994, the land has been part of Bernard and Marilyn (Turner) Campbell's Scottish Highlands Golf Course.

Eight
Route 28

The Londonderry Turnpike was constructed as a money-making venture by a group of investors organized in 1804. It was the New Hampshire portion of a 63-mile toll road between Boston and Concord which cost just over $67,000 to build and opened to the public in 1806. Salem sat at the turnpike's halfway point and its taverns and toll gates saw tremendous activity. Tolls ended before 1840 and the highway remained a dirt path until being macadamized in 1904. Horse-drawn sleighs were still typical winter transportation when this 1914 photograph was taken, looking north from Hampshire Street. In 1924, the turnpike—now called Route 28— was so deeply covered with snow that it was impassable for three months.

Back around 1920 the intersection of Lawrence Road and Route 28 was still a placid country crossroads—a fitting place to pause with a wheelbarrow and ponder the future. Just beyond the two houses is Hampshire Street, where vehicles once turned left off South Broadway for their journey to Methuen—avoiding Route 28's unpaved dip into a soggy hollow just below the MSPCA farm. Hampshire Street, with its route not yet broken by Route 213, continued on to the section still existing near today's Methuen police station.

During the summer of 1950, Route 28 was rebuilt from the Depot to the state line, replacing the two-lane, concrete road installed in 1925 with a four-lane asphalt highway. George Brox accomplished the job for just $286,000. Arthur Seed was given only three weeks to move—or lose—his house at the corner of Route 28 and Lawrence Road. He opted to move the 1834 structure up onto the hill in his backyard (304 Lawrence Road)—living in it all the while.

Evelyn Seed opened a tea room called The Birches in 1929 at the southwest corner of Route 28 and Hampshire Road. Her restaurant became a convenient and popular stop for automobile travelers on the highway. To accommodate the ever-increasing number of tourists, she soon built some of the first over-night cabins north of Boston, and later added trailers for vacationers and racetrackers. She sold the business in 1976. Twenty years later, the 3-acre site was leveled for yet another shopping plaza.

Back in the 1920s, Loeschner's Store had one of the dozen fireworks stands that sprouted every summer on the half-mile stretch of Route 28 closest to the state line. When certain sizes of fireworks were outlawed in Massachusetts, distributors got South Salem residents to set up stands from Flag Day through July Fourth. Thousands poured over the border to buy, and caseloads were sold to people on their way home from auto races at Rockingham. In 1955, Diltz Ford opened in Loeschner's old store at 500 South Broadway.

A young Joseph Sweeney performs tricks for the camera, *c.* 1958—on a swing set that today would be in the lobby of the state liquor store at 417 South Broadway. The 1892 Edward Cartwright home, where the Sweeneys lived in the 1950s, gave way to the new liquor store which opened October 18, 1965. The fields to the south are those of the Donabedian farm, much of which is now occupied by a large shopping plaza at 419 South Broadway.

The new four-lane Route 28 appeared on the cover of *New Hampshire Highways Magazine* in February 1951. Looking north from Hillcrest Road, the field at left is the current site of Ed Newman's Ford and Hyundai dealership. The billboards backed up to the house on the left are the only ones surviving in town today. In a 1964 national beautification project, President Lyndon B. Johnson's wife, Lady Bird, targeted billboards as an eye-sore and their numbers have dwindled rapidly ever since.

Most of the highway's farms have long since given way to commercial development, but Daniel Donabedian still perseveres. Standing at far right in this photograph, he showed off his brand new tractor with a friend in 1942.

Daniel's parents moved to Salem from Newburyport in 1909, at the request of Mrs. Donabedian's father, Avedis Vartanian. He had broken his leg in a fall from a vegetable wagon and needed help at the family's South Broadway farm. The Donabedians and their baby son Suren stayed on in Salem, where five more children, including Daniel, were born.

Suren and Danny Donabedian farmed about 25 acres on Route 28 and Lawrence Road, selling produce to Lawrence markets. As business grew, they also bought vegetables from outside suppliers, expanding their wholesale business. Suren has now passed away, but Danny still works the farm. His son Greg joined the business a number of years ago, continuing in his family's footsteps.

Avedis and Mary Vartanian started this South Broadway truck farm at the turn of the century. Their sons, Sam and Walter Vartanian, kept a herd of cows here back in the 1930s, but specialized in vegetables like this 1940s crop of red turban squash. Posing are, from left to right: Ginny Donabedian, unknown, Sylvia Vartanian, Arnold Vartanian, Helen Vartanian, and Shirley Donabedian. Vartanian's field later became the site of the Jerry Lewis Cinema at 451 South Broadway—Salem's first modern movie theater.

When the Depression put Albert Granz out of work, he made ends meet by sharpening lawn mowers in his Methuen basement. In 1936, he and his wife started their Route 28 business with a gas station, living at first in a one-room cabin out back. Granz was South Salem's air-raid warden during World War II, cranking his rooftop siren during blackouts to make passing cars turn off their lights. Daughter Judy, here c. 1951, now operates Granz, Inc. with her husband, Robert Yennaco, at 391 South Broadway.

Sam Consentino opened his woodworking shop at 402 South Broadway in 1946, on land his uncle had purchased from the Kealeys in 1929. Sam married the next year and added on an apartment in which he and his wife Catherine raised their five children. In 1951, a supplier suggested they add plywoods and mouldings to their line of hand-made kitchen cabinets, lawn furniture, and picket fences. The suggestion was a good one—Rockingham Lumber celebrated its 50th anniversary in 1996.

New Hampshire's notorious stand against sales and income taxes, plus lower tariffs on cigarettes and liquor, have fueled a border war with Massachusetts for decades. Lower prices have continually lured shoppers over the state line and sent them home with trunkloads of alcohol and tobacco. After Prohibition's repeal in 1933, New Hampshire seized the financial opportunity to run its own state liquor stores. Salem's first one (above) opened in 1939 at 346 South Broadway, in a building provided by town political boss, Selectman Bill Barron. Within a year, the store ranked eighth among the state's thirty-seven outlets, with sales exceeding $209,000. By the time of the 1942 photograph below, its popularity had cars parking up and down Route 28—and long lines of customers waiting their turn to get in. The present store, built in 1965 at 417 South Broadway, ranked third among fifty-one outlets in 1995, with annual sales exceeding $9.4 million.

Richard Pattee's tavern originally stood on Lawrence Road, very near today's Senter Street. Londonderry Turnpike surveyor Laommi Baldwin headquartered himself there and persuaded Pattee to move the tavern to the exciting new road. Pattee agreed, thus becoming the first to cash in on the business opportunities on Route 28.

The turnpike turned out to be everything Baldwin had promised and Pattee's establishment thrived. The tavern's most prominent guest was the General Marquis de Lafayette, who stopped in 1824 for a roast turkey dinner and libations. The property was sold to Gilman D. Kelley in 1863. His son, J. William Kelley, owned it until the fall of 1917. Today, only the main barn survives—the tallest portion of a shopping plaza at 343 South Broadway.

When J. William Kelley owned the Pattee's Tavern property, he named the place White Bridge Farm in honor of Salem's only covered bridge. It was a handsome white structure with traditional lattice-work sides, built to protect the railroad trestle that spans the Spicket just south of Kelley Road. Constructed by the Boston & Maine in 1887, it stood for thirty years. Looking north through the bridge is Kelley's Crossing, and just to the left is Benjamin Kelley's barn.

The old tavern was remodeled to this appearance after World War I. Later, Anna and Benning Noyes ran a restaurant there and started the Noyes Terrace housing development on the southeastern portion of the former farm. In 1945, Douglas A. Seed and his wife Mary bought the house, barn, and 20 acres of land for $10,000. The Seeds rented apartments upstairs and ran functions and parties in the large dining room where Lafayette had dined 125 years earlier.

In February 1951, the Seeds opened White Bridge Candies in the renovated ground floor of the barn, with the candy kitchen located in the ell. In the early 1960s, the Seeds installed a trampoline court—twelve trampolines on which guests could jump for 50¢ per half-hour. Vandals scaled the fence one night and slashed all the trampolines to ribbons. Uninsured for that particular plight, Mr. Seed promptly removed the devices and built Salem's first roadside miniature golf course in their place. One fairway was in the shape of an arrow that coincidentally pointed to the gliderport on Brady Avenue. The Seeds later learned that glider pilots often used it to quickly orient themselves to the runway!

Route 28's transformation from sleepy rural highway to busy commercial strip was helped along considerably in the 1950s by Salem Street's Paul and Veronica Garabedian. Paul started his business with one dump truck in 1934. By the time the above photograph was taken twenty-five years later, he was on his way to becoming the town's largest individual property owner. Between 1955 and 1958, Garabedian constructed three buildings across from Kelley Road. They housed Butcher Boy, Tasty Treat Bakery, Alan's Restaurant, and Simons—Salem's first discount department store. A year later, he built the town's first modern supermarket, called Samsons (below, at right). Howard Johnson's opened next door at 374 South Broadway in 1962. Its building, also constructed by Garabedian, housed Lancer Steak House for a short time after Howard Johnson's left. Since 1972, however, it has been home to Bob Loo's Restaurant.

For years, Route 28 crossed the Spicket River between Kelley Road and Seed Street via this World War I Veterans Memorial Bridge, built in 1919. The river has been moved and squeezed many times. It once ran very near Route 28 across from Kelley Road—until it was pushed east some 300 feet in the 1950s to create more land for stores and shopping plazas. When Interstate 93 was built in 1960, the Spicket was straightened into a virtual canal for its last half-mile flow into Methuen.

During the Christmas week of 1949, Roland LaRochelle and his father, Wilfred LaRochelle, moved their kitchen cabinet business from Lawrence to Route 28 in Salem. Roland purchased the land between Doris Court and the Spicket River from the Fiola family, who had run a sawmill and a Crosley automobile dealership on the site. With the post-war housing boom, the LaRochelles' cabinet business soared and, in the next thirty-five years, they would build on eighteen additions! Since Roland's retirement, his son Paul has managed the property as twenty retail rental units. This is the way the complex appeared in the late 1950s.

Hurricane Edna visited Salem in September 1954—flooding Route 28 as the Spicket overflowed its banks. When the turnpike was laid out in 1804, low lands between the river and Kelley Road dictated that the highway be turned slightly west between those two points. The resulting jog, still in the road today, has probably saved the area from flooding to a much greater degree on many occasions.

Kelley Road (left) was laid out in 1752 as a toll road. Its intersection with Route 28 is shown here as it looked in 1920. From 1806 until almost 1840, Route 28 was also a toll road. A penny bought a mile of travel for ten sheep, ten swine, or a horse and rider. Anyone caught leaving the highway to avoid paying was charged a triple-the-toll penalty.

Salem's first modern fast-food emporium was the A & W Root Beer Drive-In, located where Newman's Plaza parking lot is today. It was followed in 1963 by Howdy Beefburger, operated by Maurice Needle at the southwest corner of Route 28 and Kelley Road. With its 15¢ burgers and 12¢ fries, Howdy's boomed—until 1966, when McDonalds opened less than a mile away. Howdy's went out of business in 1968 and the site was later occupied by a Jack-in-the-Box restaurant.

In 1955 Daniel and William Yameen posed cheerfully inside their new Butcher Boy meat market at 315 South Broadway. They faced some competition in the early years from a store called Meatland next door, but the Yameens won out, attracting customers from as far away as Boston. For decades, a proper shopping pilgrimage to Salem included stops at Kealey Farms, the liquor store—and Butcher Boy. Today Kealey's is gone, but Butcher Boy still tops lots of shopping lists.

Back in the early 1950s, the only place to buy a Volkswagen in the Merrimack Valley was at Doug Bradley's combination gas station and car dealership on Route 28 in Salem. Called Continental Motors, it was one of the first VW dealers in New England. Jack Harrison and Arthur Park bought the business in 1959, moving it to Lawrence three years later. The Littlewood family then opened their Atomic Sub shop in the building, which was located midway between Cluff Road and Veterans Memorial Drive.

Looking up Route 28 from just above Westchester Street in 1926, the north corner of the 6,000-foot oval board track at the Rockingham Motor Speedway fills the view west of the highway. From 1925 to 1929, this track was as popular as the famous auto track at Indianapolis—only newer and faster! See this book's companion volume, *Salem, NH, Vol. II: Trolleys, Canobie Lake, and Rochkingham Park*, for the full story of auto racing at Rockingham.

These two houses, and several more like them, once stood side by side on the west side of South Broadway near the Depot. Instead of living life to the sound of screeching brakes and beeping horns, their residents listened to the clickety-clack of wagon wheels and horses' hoofs. Members of the Norris family (above) lived in their Route 28 house from 1884 until 1933. When Eunice Baker married Frank Norris in 1916, small numbers of automobiles were just beginning to travel the highway. Eunice was paid by the state to sit in the front window of the house and count each auto that passed by. She reportedly received a penny per car; unfortunately for her, the average daily traffic count was far short of today's 22,000 vehicles! Pictured above c. 1911 are, from left to right: (seated) Ida Allen, Susan Norris, and Hiram Norris; (standing) Grace Norris, Weston Norris, Gertrude Norris Webb, and Frank Norris.

Brothers Clemens O. Seifert (above) and Charles A. Seifert brought their Coca-Cola bottling plant to town in 1921. Charles had almost twenty years experience with the product by then, getting his start at a bottling company in New Bern, North Carolina, back in 1903. By 1919, he had formed a company to purchase the bottling franchise in Haverhill, moving it to Salem two years later. It didn't take the Seifert family long to become active participants in the community. Clemens ran the Salem plant in its early years and soon was also coaching baseball at Woodbury High. Selling Coca-Cola here was something of a challenge at first. People loved their Moxie and their root beer, and were slow to develop a taste for the secret formula from Atlanta.

Coca-Cola had its roots in a wine-based beverage called Vin Mariani—so popular by 1885 that everyone from the Pope to the President was drinking it. Atlanta pharmacist John Sythe Pemberton mixed up a pirated version of the drink, replacing the wine with sugar and caffeine. He called his new syrup Coca-Cola and sold it as a stimulating elixir to be taken straight or mixed with water. Its name was derived from two of the original ingredients—the coca leaf (cocaine) and the kola nut (caffeine). Oh, how stimulating it must have been! Pemberton sold his secret formula and, in 1892, Asa G. Candler and two partners founded the Coca-Cola Company. When Candler had the idea to mix his syrup with carbonated water, a phenomenon was born.

118

The Salem Coca-Cola Bottling Company got its start in this building, which is still part of the 23 South Broadway plant today. Fred Herbst, a brother-in-law of the Seiferts, succeeded Clemens as manager, living in the house that once stood just north of the plant. That house was home to a number of relatives and employees over the years. Back in the early 1950s, when one of its apartments was empty, the company even drew names out of a hat to see which worker would win the right to move in. Ernest Shaw (below, left) was the plant superintendent until his death in 1964. Also included in the 1940s photograph are Fred Johnston (second from the right)—who later managed the company's Manchester plant—and Joe Batal (third from right). Charles A.'s son, Charles W. Seifert, came to Salem in 1933, and was succeeded by his son-in-law, Bill Hamblett, in 1970. The business was sold in 1982 to a company funded by Japanese interests.

Jim Sayer's Ole Rock Drive-In Theatre was built on the site of today's post office in the early 1950s. Its biggest hit ever was a 1954 Jane Russell film called *The French Line*. Banned in Manchester, the 3-D movie brought lines of cars to Salem to hear Russell deliver the immortal line, "I'm Gonna Pop All the Corn in Nebraska." The Ole Rock was the town's second drive-in. The first was on Playcamp Road, operated by the Weinhold family .

In November 1954 trees lined North Broadway, a huge bell hung in the square, and the town Christmas tree was about to be placed near the picket fence at far left, where the Pilgrim Block previously stood. The flat-topped Sullivan Block (left) once housed Salem's telephone operators and the Depot's post office. In 1972, Republicans and Democrats had side-by-side headquarters in the two first-floor store fronts. Built in the early 1920s, the building burned in the early 1970s.

William Croft (at right) came to Salem in 1907 to join Thomas Devine in forming the Granite State Potato Chip Company in this building at 227 North Broadway. Additions were soon added, as the scent of freshly cooked chips wafted over Route 28, attracting thousands of customers. The company's trademark was registered in Washington in 1917 and is the first known use of the Old Man of the Mountains in advertising.

William Croft became the sole owner in 1917, when Granite State chips were still sold only at the factory. Soon, Clarence W. and Charles E. Merrill, J.A. Dion, and Henry Boudreau signed on to service other retail outlets as independent distributors. They are shown here c. 1932 with new trucks they bought to cover delivery routes stretching as far west as Worcester. Today, the ninety-year-old manufacturing business is still in the family, now being run by the fourth Croft generation named William.

It's interesting that Methuen's three most famous millionaires all had Salem connections. Edward F. Searles once owned almost 10 percent of Salem, including Rockingham Park. David Nevins, who would become an owner of Lawrence's ill-fated Pemberton mill in 1854, was born in a house on North Policy Street.

Charles H. Tenney (shown here) grew up in Salem, at the tavern his father ran on a portion of the Londonderry Turnpike now called Old Rockingham Road. After attending the No. 6 School, Charles grew up to run the Tenney hat factory on Broadway in Methuen, then moved on to New York where he had one of the world's largest hat exporting businesses. He built Grey Court, a hilltop castle in Methuen, and bought back his boyhood farm in Salem.

Today's Old Rockingham Road originally comprised the northernmost stretch of Salem's Route 28. Traffic crossed the railroad tracks at Gage's Crossing (just above the chip factory) and continued on to Mason's Store—where two 90° turns and another railroad crossing were required. For safety's sake the highway was rerouted to its current location east of the tracks in the early 1930s. Because the new road divided Tenney's farm, this bridge was provided to allow his cows to get to pasture. It was torn down in 1960.

After Charles Tenney purchased his boyhood home, which included some 200 acres of land, he used the property to breed and raise prize Guernseys. This ad for the farm ran in 1925, when his son, Daniel G. Tenney, owned the property. The land was eventually sold and the barn was demolished. The bull ring building was converted into a home at 45 Old Rockingham Road. The old tavern house still stands across the street at No. 48, strategically located near the Londonderry Turnpike's halfway point between Boston and Concord.

123

Taken in 1962 from a point now roughly over Salem High School, this aerial view, looking west of Route 28 (bottom), holds many interesting details.

Starting at bottom center and going clockwise, the field with the L-shaped road was Paul Garabedian's golf driving range in the early 1960s; it's now the site of Frank Geary's Park View Motel. The Rockingham Mall was still ten years away and Rockingham Park Boulevard ended at Route 28. The Veteran's Memorial Parkway was not yet built. Interstate 93's Exit 1 had no ramps to accommodate traffic to or from the north, since it was planned that Exit 2, Main Street, and Pleasant Street would handle the race traffic from Manchester. The pasture land in the upper left is Turner's Mountain View farm, which became the Scottish Highlands Golf Course in 1994. And in the space between Pleasant Street and the racing oval, the giant shopping mall would still be thirty years in the future.

124

Continuing clockwise, acres and acres of trees cover land that would eventually support bustling industrial parks and housing developments. At bottom right, Sayer's Ole Rock Drive-In Theater is across from the track's Route 28 entrance—next to Bob Nault's auto junk yard and Cain's Trailer Park. Today, the post office and First N.H. Bank are on the site of the Drive-In, and the Weathervane Restaurant occupies the site of the junk yard.

In the center of it all is world-famous Rockingham Park. Opened briefly in 1906 as a horse-racing track, it later became an aerodrome and then a top-notch automobile race track. Legalized betting brought Rockingham back to life as a horse track in 1933 and the park still thrives today. A complete history of New England's first and finest thoroughbred race track is contained in this book's companion volume, *Salem, NH, Vol. II: Trolleys, Canobie Lake, and Rockingham Park*.

At the turn of the century, the nation was honeycombed with a network of electric streetcar lines, allowing Americans a new freedom and ease of travel never-before experienced. Almost every trolley system had an amusement park, built by a trolley company to stimulate summer and weekend ridership.

Salem's trolley park was built at Canobie Lake in 1902. The Hudson, Pelham & Salem Street Railway (part of a larger system serving northeastern Massachusetts and southern New Hampshire) ran from Haverhill to Nashua on its east-west routes, and from Lawrence to Canobie Lake Park on its north-south lines. There were other trolley parks in the region, too—Pine Island in Manchester, Laveview in Dracut, and the Hampton and Salisbury beaches. But Canobie was all ours. Generations hold fond memories of working and playing at what seemed like our own personal amusement park!

This fuzzy 1950s bird's-eye view of Canobie Lake Park shows the large trolley loop (at far left). It was once lined with double tracks that carried trolley-loads of passengers to and from the park. After the demise of the streetcars in 1929, the loop, which entered from Brookdale Road, carried buses into the resort. It was not until after World War I that any facilities were provided for automobiles, since Canobie's primary goal was to generate streetcar revenues.

From the 1930s through the 1950s, Canobie's dance hall showcased a stream of music industry giants including Glenn Miller, the Dorseys, and Benny Goodman. In the 1960s, the next generation danced to the Beach Boys, Gene Pitney, Sonny and Cher, and many more. Canobie's first century is completely chronicled in this book's companion volume, *Salem, NH, Vol. II: Trolleys, Canobie Lake, and Rockingham Park.*

Acknowledgments

A work of this type would be impossible to complete without the help and generosity of the entire community. The authors would like to give special thanks to the following: the Salem Historical Society, Louise Ackerman, Ernest Mack, Carol McShane, the Jack Lahey Collection, Guy Ackerman, James A. Sayer Jr., the Raymond Lundberg family, Steve Barbin, Buddy Winiarz, and Christine Willis.

We also wish to express our gratitude to the following individuals, organizations, and businesses who have provided photographs and/or other assistance in the creation of this book: Mary Seed, Mabel Dyke, Harry Azarian, Arthur Railton, Lelia Rowell, Lester Hall, Doris Lamprey, Margaret Robbins, Bill Ermer, Bob Stone, America's Stonehenge, Eunice Sharpe Girard, Peg Akroyd, Charlotte Lundberg Blinn, Mr. and Mrs. Robert Mason Jr., Ruby Smith, Rich Demerle, Ruth Levesque, Rita Hamel, Helen Berube, Donald Boland, James Falls, Sam Zannini, Mr. and Mrs. Daniel Donabedian, Edwin Kulesz, Clarence Merrill, Carlton Parker, Irene Drouin, the Methuen Historic Commission, Dan Gagnon, Naomi Ireland, Juliet George, Edward Manoogian, Alice Dietrich, Gordon Collupy, Ruth Henning, Mr. and Mrs. Al Greenwood, Claire Pappalardo, Wally Craig, George Gelt, Syliva Gelt Bonaccorso, David Hicks, Mr. and Mrs. John Hicks, John Castricone, Mr. and Mrs. Frederick Detlefs, Joseph Sweeney, Doris Sweeney, Pauline Keith, Kenneth Norris, Floyd Norris, Jill Goundrey Moe, Mr. and Mrs. Robert D. Goundrey, Ken Skulski of the Immigrant City Archives, Ned Lagana, Sandra Roulston, Rita Wefers, O.R. Cummings, the Paul Garabedian Jr. family, Marie Leone, Fred Barone, Mr. and Mrs. Andrew Pellerin, Donald Turner, Mr. and Mrs. William Blaine, Alice Dahood, Helen Voskerjian, Mr. and Mrs. William Troy, Stephanie Belko, Maurice Needle, John Sullivan, John Packard, Dorothy Doyle, Krista McLeod, the Nevins Memorial Library, Judy Granz Yennaco, Tina Gagnon, Joan Schoenenburger, Spectrum Business Service, Mr. and Mrs. Sam Consentino, the New Hampshire State Liquor Commission, the *Eagle Tribune*, Stephanie Micklon, Paul LaRochelle, Roland LaRochelle, Fred Scott, Pamela Yameen, Loris White, Ruth Turner, Mr. and Mrs. Bernard W. Campbell, Kevin Campbell, William "Buddy" Croft, Mr. and Mrs. Robert Thomas, the Holland Family Collection, Jeff Barraclough, Nadine Morison, Pat Keegan, Mary Troy, John Troy, Margie Troy, Mr. and Mrs. Joshua Smith, the Kelley Library, Michael Jacobsen, the New Hampshire Good Roads Association, Bill Boynton, the New Hampshire Department of Transportation, the Walker Transportation Collection—Beverly, MA Historical Society, the Harry A. Frye Collection, Dartmouth College, Harriet Headley, Charles "Buddy" Nelson, Ronald Belanger, Barbara Heim, Beverly Connell, Marjorie Jackson, Dorothy Morrill, George E. Merrill, Marion Cullen, Barbara Lessard, Joan Sabatini, Robert Chute, Mary Boland, Mary Turner Somma, Eddie Turner Jr., Genevieve Turner, Mr. and Mrs. William Hamblett, Frank Conley, Bill Grace, Dave Davidson, William Woodbury, Lawrence Belair, *The Beacon Magazine*, Richard Noyes, Edgar Gilbert, and Arthur Mueller Jr. of the *Salem Observer*.